Productivity Gainsharing

Brian E. Graham-Moore is a professor of management at the University of Texas at Austin.

Timothy L. Ross is director of the BG Productivity and Gainsharing Institute and professor of accounting at Bowling Green State University in Bowling Green, Ohio.

Both authors have extensive experience in research and consulting on productivity gainsharing. They are co-authors of the highly successful *Scanlon Way to Improved Productivity*.

PRODUCTIVITY GAINSHARING

How Employee Incentive Programs Can Improve Business Performance

BRIAN E. GRAHAM-MOORE
TIMOTHY L. ROSS

A SPECTRUM BOOK

Prentice-Hall, Inc., Englewood Cliffs, New Jersey 07632

Library of Congress Cataloging in Publication Data

Main entry under title:

Productivity gainsharing.

"A Spectrum Book."
Bibliography: p.
Includes index.
1. Gain sharing—Addresses, essays, lectures.
I. Graham-Moore, Brian E. (date). II. Ross, Timothy L. (date).
HD4928.G34P76 1983 658.3'225 83-3250
ISBN 0-13-725051-7
ISBN 0-13-725044-4 (pbk.)

This book is available at a special discount when ordered in bulk quantities. Contact Prentice-Hall, Inc., General Publishing Division, Special Sales, Englewood Cliffs, N.J. 07632.

A Spectrum Book. Printed in the United States of America.

Figure 9-1. Lawler, *Pay and Organization Development*, © 1981. Addison-Wesley, Reading, MA. Reprinted with permission.

10 9 8 7 6 5 4 3 2 1

ISBN 0-13-725051-7

ISBN 0-13-725044-4 {PBK.}

Editorial/production supervision by Norma G. Ledbetter
Cover design © 1983 by Jeannette Jacobs
Manufacturing buyer: Cathie Lenard

Prentice-Hall International, Inc., *London*
Prentice-Hall of Australia Pty. Limited, *Sydney*
Prentice-Hall Canada Inc., *Toronto*
Prentice-Hall of India Private Limited, *New Delhi*
Prentice-Hall of Japan, Inc., *Tokyo*
Prentice-Hall of Southeast Asia Pte. Ltd., *Singapore*
Whitehall Books Limited, *Wellington, New Zealand*
Editora Prentice-Hall do Brasil Ltda., *Rio de Janeiro*

Contents

Foreword

Democracy and rewarding individuals according to their contribution are two fundamental American values. In most American work places, however, neither of these has traditionally been true. People have not been given a say in important work place decisions that affect them nor have they been rewarded according to their contribution. This incongruence between traditional American values and the way organizations are managed has not been seriously challenged nor has it had disastrous consequences for the country until recently. Increasingly it is becoming apparent that something needs to be done to correct the situation. American productivity may be suffering as a consequence of our failure to motivate people by rewarding them for their performance and as a result of not utilizing their ideas and thoughts toward improving organizational effectiveness.

The challenge is to define approaches that will allow people to participate and that will tie their rewards to their performance. There is ample evidence in research literature that when this occurs people will be more productive and the society will be healthier.

Productivity gainsharing is a long well-established American approach to combining participative management and reward for performance. Unfortunately, until recently it has not been widely used. Despite numerous success stories it remains a curiosity in the United States rather than a widely disseminated and heavily utilized approach to better management. Despite a recent increase in interest, there is no question that productivity gainsharing has been and still is dramatically underutilized. The record of its success is impressive, and there is every reason to believe that with wider adoption productivity gainsharing will be even more successful. It represents an important American approach to creating organizations that are competitive in the international arena.

This book provides a much-needed, very timely guide to productivity gainsharing. The last ten years have seen the increasing adoption of gainsharing programs by major U.S. corporations. Today Owens-Illinois, General Electric, DANA, TRW, and others mentioned in the book have adopted gainsharing with considerable success. In many respects it seems as if gainsharing is an idea whose time has come.

This book should be an important contribution to the spread of gainsharing. It not only reports on some of the successes with gainsharing, but also it tackles the often difficult issue of formula construction in a way that is both understandable and comprehensive. In addition, it attacks several of the most important issues with respect to the spread of gainsharing; in particular it looks at the issue of gainsharing in service organizations. With the economy in the United States shifting more toward service, it is particularly important that gainsharing models be developed that are applicable to an array of service institutions. So far, gainsharing has largely been tried in manufacturing environments and proved successful. What is needed now are methods that widen its applicability.

Unlike many articles and books concerned with the mechanics of pay incentive plans, this book focuses on both the organization design and culture issues that are involved in gainsharing and formula construction. All too often the organizational issues are ignored, and organizations are preoccupied with formula construction. The behavioral side of gainsharing is at least as important as the formula side, and thus I am particularly pleased to see that this book gives coverage to the organizational behavior issues involved in gainsharing.

Overall it seems clear that the United States is moving toward more participative and democratic approaches to management. Some organizations have moved in this direction without making dramatic changes in the area of rewards. This may be a viable strategy, but, as this book points out and my experience certainly indicates, ultimately an organization has to turn its attention to the reward systems. To the person who is interested in combining participative management and gainsharing, this book should be an important resource.

Edward E. Lawler III

Director, Center for
Effective Organizations,
The University of Southern California

Preface

In the past five years, information on productivity gainsharing and organizational development has grown dramatically. Indeed, this growth of information has been helpful in the transformation of the relationship between employers and employees. For those firms with productivity gainsharing, this transformation was aided by the healthy sharing of risk. That is, productivity gainsharing reinforces positively whether or not a bonus is earned because identity is being developed with the firm. This is one of the uniquely valuable aspects of productivity gainsharing. To communicate how and why gainsharing has this value is the objective of this book. Indeed, this book attempts to fill the void in the literature that exists between simple "one-shot" case studies and overly sophisticated academic analyses. It is time to synthesize productivity gainsharing into a theoretical focus and begin to specify how employees, managers, and other decision makers can use this information.

This book is based on the premise that understanding all aspects of productivity gainsharing while understanding the needs of the organization is the only way to integrate this form of incentive system into an organization. Unfortunately, in this world of lists, many people would prefer a list of dos and don'ts on how to accomplish this goal. Instead of a list, Chapter 1 deals with the theoretical aspects of productivity gainsharing and organizational development. It can be readily seen that there is no simple checklist, yet there does exist a framework for fitting productivity gainsharing into the appropriate organizational context.

For the uninitiated, Chapter 2 brings them up to date on the vast literature on productivity gainsharing. Indeed, there has been an explosion of new works in the area as well as innovations such as Improshare. In order to grasp the principles of productivity gainsharing, a comprehensive review of significant studies is offered there. Chapter 3 continues to flesh out the principles of the relationship between productivity gainsharing formulas and organizational development that was introduced in Chapter 2. Chapters 4 and 5 provide longitudinal and case evidence of real firms with solid experience with productivity gainsharing. These chapters attempt to provide a theoretical focus while providing descriptive information.

Chapters 6, 7, and 8 deal with totally new ground. Because incentives are rarely used in the construction industry, for example, a Delphi study by Alex Laufer was designed and carried out to raise the question, "What if incentives were available?" Chapter 7 deals with the important issues of productivity gainsharing and the service industries. For years, most successful productivity gainsharing firms have been manufacturers. Thus, many persons have believed these forms of incentives would work only there. Warren Hauck and Tim Ross dispel that notion rather handily. Chapter 8 deals with the foremost issue of organization development — that is, of organizational development. One can readily see that if productivity gainsharing and other forms of quality-of-work interventions are to last, how do they become institutionalized? Paul Goodman and James Dean offer an insightful, thought-provoking discussion that all decision makers in this area should read.

Failure issues are discussed in Chapter 9 by Tim Ross. The examples chosen for this chapter reflect prototypical principles and the issues of why some plans inevitably fail. Indeed, managers should probably read this chapter first because productivity gainsharing has never been for everyone. For example, a common belief of managers of productivity gainsharing is that it makes "good managers manage better." Last, Chapter 10 is our attempt to take a look into the future. We suggest in Chapter 1 that newer forms of gainsharing will evolve, and this book ends on that note. We believe, for example, that the future of gainsharing is exceptionally bright. There is more emphasis on productivity nationally — especially to beat the Japanese challenge that Professor William Ouchi has depicted so well. We know that better information, knowledge, and experience are available on gainsharing. Indeed, more plans have been installed in the past three years than in the last 15. Today, there is a more cooperative labor environment. Given the right conditions and management commitment, productivity gainsharing significantly increases productivity and the quality of work life.

No book is the solitary effort of the authors. Both of us have seen our material grow in the courses we offer at Bowling Green State University and The University of Texas at Austin. Our students and colleagues have patiently listened to our ideas and have offered valued criticism. Chapter 4 owes a great debt of gratitude to DeSoto Chemical Corporation and their most valued resource — their fine personnel. Without the sharing of their time and thoughts, this longitudinal case could not have been written. Indeed, we are grateful to all the firms and their personnel that have contributed to this fund of knowledge. John Hunger of Prentice-Hall patiently coaxed this project to its fruition. The quality of the final version of this manuscript reflects the care and precision of the production staff of the General Publishing Division of Prentice-Hall.

Most important in projects of this type are the support, help, and encouragement one receives from family and friends. Our grateful thanks to Robin Graham-Moore and Ruthann Ross. They endured this project with remarkable grace.

Grateful acknowledgment is given to the following for granting permission to reprint material.

Chapter 3, "PG Formulas: Developing a Reward Structure to Achieve Organization Goals" (with Brian E. Graham-Moore), by Max Bazerman, Assistant Professor, School of Management, Boston University, Boston, MA.

Chapter 6, "PG and the Construction Industry: A Delphi Study," by Alexander Laufer, Civil Engineering Department, Texas A&M University, College Station, Texas.

Chapter 7, "Is PG Applicable to Service Sector Firms?" (with Timothy L. Ross), by Warren C. Hauck.

Chapter 8, "Making Productivity Programs Last," by Paul S. Goodman, Professor of Management, Graduate School of Industrial Administration, Carnegie-Mellon University, and by James W. Dean, Jr., Ph.D., Assistant Professor of Organizational Behavior, College of Business Administration, The Pennsylvania State University.

Productivity Gainsharing

1

Introduction to PG:
A Theoretical Model

by Brian E. Graham-Moore and Timothy L. Ross

Productivity gainsharing (PG) has a long, informal history. Some forms of PG can be traced back to ancient Rome. Any time an owner/manager shared a bonus with workers that was caused by their increased effort, skill, and/or luck, PG was a possibility. Because human capital was invested along with nonhuman capital to increase worth, it occurred to some owner/managers that an unmeasured contribution was being made by the human resource. Although wages were fully intended to compensate the human resource, it became obvious that wages were not directly tied to productivity.

Then, as well as more recently, a fair wage was aimed at the average worker for standard (average) output. With this concept of fairness, an employer is paying most workers fairly while overpaying low producers and underpaying high producers. The pay target, once established, is aimed squarely at standard output, average workers, or acceptable performance. It surprises no one that out of initial concern for fairness, employers created static reward systems, not dynamic ones. They paid for expected productivity at each rung of an imagined sturdy ladder. If performance was higher than a particular pay rung, then only by paying at the next rung (promotion or step increase) could pay be matched with performance. Also, managers discovered that if performance was lower than a particular pay rung, it was difficult to move the worker down to the lower rung on the ladder.

Partially in response to matching individual differences to the dynamics of tying pay (or a portion of it) to performance, individual incentives were created. Dysfunctional consequences arose. Competition rather than cooperation was reinforced. Hoarding of materials and tightly controlling work methods became common behavior among workers. If tasks were interdependent rather than wholly autonomous, task arrangements interfered with individual incentives.

A general decline of individual incentive systems has been occurring over the past 20 years. Less than 22% of American manufacturers report they use individual incentives.

It seems, however, that the process of matching individual or group performance with equitable rewards, once begun, never ends. That is, there exists a need recognized by managers to stimulate productivity by tying in some reward with the dynamic fluctuation of productivity. A wide variety of socioeconomic systems has been developed to deal with the rather basic functions of reward systems.

The simplest way to frame this question is: Who gets what? How are they going to get it? And will what they get be a fair motivator? Although anthropologists, economists, psychologists, and sociologists have focused their research on contemporary workers in an attempt to answer these questions from their various perspectives, their research efforts so far have produced no more than descriptive accounts of the phenomenon of PG.

WHY IS PG RELATIVELY RARE?

The historical occurrence of PG has never explained why some managers and workers evolve to PG, accept it, and use it while other managers and workers eschew it. Why do the needs, aspirations, values, and motivations of some managers and workers permit PG to come about? Indeed, what are the variables associated with PG? What intensity and mix of these variables seem to establish successful PG?

The time is ripe to shed light on the phenomenon of PG because of the national need for increased productivity. Also, the disciplines involved in explaining PG have never been in a better state to achieve understanding of PG while enlightening society. Multivariate assessment methods combined with appropriate theory should produce findings that indicate the profile of variables associated with different forms of PG success.

We believe in the value of the scientific method as applied to PG. Sufficient understanding already exists about the law of supply and demand to set prices. Sufficient understanding exists about personality and culture to explain character structure in many societies. Sufficient understanding exists to measure IQ and use it in personnel selection. And sufficient understanding exists about social class to predict intergenerational socioeconomic status (and who *really* gets what and why at a macro level). Given these contributions to understanding by social science (the "soft" disciplines), no apology is necessary for the lack of understanding of PG that stems from lack of method. That is, the precision we need for understand and predicting PG is well within the state of the art of the behavioral sciences.

THE CURRENT LACK
OF A THEORY

PG has evolved over many years without all-encompassing attention. Only one or two dimensions of PG have been scrutinized as research topics. At best, PG has received narrowly focused attention from the disciplines of industrial relations and organizational psychology. Thus, it may be useful to review some context before developing a theory.

One of the best-known PG plans, for example, was founded in the 1940s by Joe Scanlon, who presumably invented it. Although he never claimed authorship, his name won't go away. It became the generic name for this type of plan. This proved widely acceptable, but it belies the fact that Joe Scanlon had never heard of the Nunn-Bush Shoe Company of Milwaukee, which installed its PG plan in 1935. Indeed, when this innovation was finally documented, it was written up as a business case 26 years after its inception!

There are two points to be made here:

1. New ideas are often old ideas, but careful scholarship can remedy that.
2. Numerous case studies are good for description in that they are readily understandable. (They usually have a beginning, middle and end.)

However, case studies almost always stand alone in the PG literature. They are hard to generalize from because they are a sample of one and require that readers perform an analysis in their minds that defies the multivariate dimensions of PG.

For example, the underlying variables associated with flight are best learned as carefully validated propositions whose interrelationships explains flight. Conversely, plowing through the fascinating case of the Wright brothers might explain flight but limit the explanation to their experience, their equipment, and so on. Generalizing from the Wrights, we might assume that all planes have rudders in front of their wings.

We, as authors, cannot proclaim that case studies are useless. After all, we write case studies. However, the ways in which case studies are constructed can enhance the value of the information we take from them.

For example, cases that employ standard measures offer better information about the variables measured. Comparisons along critical dimensions are more useful. Categorizations of findings seem more possible and generalization appears more likely.

Where does this leave us? We could continue with the narrow disciplinary studies of the past and hope that someday someone connects pertinent information from diverse sources. We could also continue to rely on good scholarship to separate new from old. And, of course, we could continue writing case studies with improved standards. Or, we can specify necessary theory and build a model to encompass the relevant factors factors of PG—in all of its manifestations.

THE THEORETICAL MODEL

Any model purports to capture relevant variables and then manipulate them to produce results. From electronic chess games to autopilots, black box models can calculate and report more quickly and rationally than their inventors can. Yet, if we invent a model for explaining PG in all its forms and under all circumstances of organizational life, our black box becomes gargantuan. Thus, one of the goals of a theoretical model is to parsimoniously express relevant, key variables that explain the initial acceptance of PG and the institutionalization of PG over time. Since this theoretical model hasn't existed up to now, we offer the following framework for a model. The specifications are based on current research on productivity and reward systems. The specifications are also based on our best judgment, derived from our consulting experience, as to which variables are perceived to be relevant.

Figure 1-1 depicts the context surrounding the PG Model. Over time the leaders of nearly all organizations attempt to understand the variables that influence productivity. If they can control or influence these variables, then they can use them in the kinds of decision making and policy formation that increase the chances for higher productivity. Figure 1-1 charts one organization on two axes—productivity and time. It shows an organization that has improved its productivity. Within the figure the letters A, B, C, and D represent the macro theoretical variables we believe must be understood by PG-oriented organizations.

PG Variables and their Interaction

At the macro level the letter A refers to organizational variables that influence the installation, upgrading, and institutionalization of PG. This variable lies inside the box of Figure 1-1 because all of its subvariables are within the control of the organization or, at least, within the scope of the

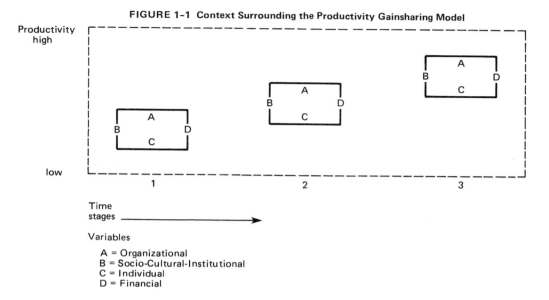

FIGURE 1-1 Context Surrounding the Productivity Gainsharing Model

Productivity
high

low

Time
stages

Variables

A = Organizational
B = Socio-Cultural-Institutional
C = Individual
D = Financial

organization's understanding. If we look at the subvariables of the macro-organizational variable *A*, they are:

1. *Climate:* perceptions and attitudes toward immediate supervision, work groups, management, and the abstract organization.
2. *Size:* the sheer and mere influence of the number of employees allowed in work groups.
3. *Technology:* the interface between the human-resource and the technical requirements of work, from machine-paced work to the know-how required that influences this interface.
4. *Policy:* the stated and implied rules on procedures that guide and constrain action.
5. *Reward structure:* the formal and informal system for reinforcing behavior valued by the organization, including its recent cumulative reward history.
6. *Identity:* the merging or convergence of individual goals and needs with those of the organizations into a congruent pattern of attitudes, beliefs, and actions.

In Figure 1-1 the letter *B* refers to the socio-cultural-institutional variables that influence PG. Notice that *B* is placed on the boundary of the organization. This is because *B* variables exist both inside and outside the boundaries of an organization. Theoretically, socio-cultural-institutional variables are distinct from purely organizational variables—in that they are not under the control of the organization.

5

There is no more diffuse and difficult class of variables to describe and understand than the socio-cultural-institutional. Nevertheless, their importance alone requires their specification. And we believe research findings and assessment strategies provide more than a ray of hope for PG-oriented firms. Therefore, if we look at subdimensions of these variables of *B*, they are:

1. *Union and industrial relations:* the degree to which one places the organization on a continuum of adversary/harmony relations existing between the firm and bargaining units.
2. *Workforce characteristics:* the demographic and cultural profile of worker groups, supervisors, and managers, especially their attitudes and values toward work in general.
3. *External environment:* the relevant exogenous variables that have long-range impact on the firm, such as geography, labor markets, housing, schools, etc.

The letter *C* in Figure 1–1 indicates all the individual-level variables that affect productivity generally and PG specifically. Each of us has individual characteristics that differentiate us from others. But which individual-level variables truly influence organizational productivity? One could honestly answer, "Any and all individual variables." However, no assessment strategy could deal with this and, theoretically, there is good reason that the following variables of *C* are more important than others:

1. *Managerial philosophy:* beliefs about how people are to be controlled and how this control is to be communicated.
2. *Trust:* one's degree of confidence in the honesty, goodness, and fairness of others.
3. *Locus of control:* degree to which an individual perceives his or her behavior can influence rewards.
4. *Skill level:* the capabilities of an individual to get results from data, people, or materials.
5. *Motivation:* the amount of force or energy an individual expends in a controlled, directed manner.
6. *Satisfaction:* the degree of contentment, gratification, and good feeling that stems from the job intrinsically or is derived from the job extrinsically.

The fourth and last macrovariable in Figure 1–1 is letter *D*, the financial variables affecting PG organizations. *D*, like *B*, is on the boundary of the organization. Factors outside of the firm, often at a national, if not international, level, can have profound effect on raw materials or final markets. Also, factors internal to the firm also can have a profound effect—

although with possibly more control. The theoretical model requires clear specification of all seemingly understandable, relevant variables of D:

1. *Internal system attributes:* accuracy, utilization, and control of inventory; production; budgets; and standards.
2. *External system attributes;* knowledge of competition, markets, pricing, economic factors, and governmental constraints.

To sum up Figure 1-1, four macro-level variables clearly influence the potential for PG—at any level of implementation. All four macrovariables interact with each other in ways that are not fully understood. The strategy of managerial leadership is to understand, as fully as possible, how each of these variables influences PG alone and in concert for the particular organization and organizational goals.

Profile

The particular profile of weight or emphasis on these variables changes with an organization's circumstances. That is, we firmly believe these variables are important, but specific profiles for success or failure depend greatly on the degree of PG a firm can optimize as well as the firm's temporal placement. That is, some firms don't meet the minimum requirements for PG and should avoid it. Other firms can handle well above the minimum and should match the PG profile to its organizational characteristics. Thus, not striving for the correct level of PG can contribute to failure as well as not meeting the minimum profile for a given PG plan. Also, attempting organizational change through PG without paying very careful attention to the history of the firm and what it hopes its future to be ignores the profound influence of growth, maturation, and time.

The discussion that follows takes an example through the theoretical model and attempts to exercise the model's capabilities as a predictive device. For simplicity's sake, not all suggested microvariables and their measurements are utilized. While a complete example of an assessment strategy is possible to provide, it might be viewed as too lengthy for discussion here. Before we begin the example a proviso is in order. The PG model is normative. It reflects all the "should-be's" we firmly believe will facilitate installation and institutionalization of PG. A complete assessment methodology is well within the state of the art. Remember, however, this model is normative. That is, it reflects all the should be's we firmly believe will facilitate installation and institutionalization of PG.

An Example

A small manufacturer is unhappy with its declining share of market and its eroding productivity. A casual look at the competition reveals that relatively it is only marginally better than it was four years ago. This firm can neither afford great investments in capital expenditures nor would it seek a buyer because the price for the firm today is less than what it was in real dollars four years ago.

Management is aware of various forms of PG and finds itself willing to review a variety of approaches to PG. It decides to assess itself, the firm, and the workers to develop information on which some form of PG will be best suited for their needs. The company is currently without any flexible reward structure other than what it hopes are competitive wages. It is very unwilling to increase wages without a true increase in productivity, as this will decrease profitability.

In our theoretical model, this company is at stage 1 of Figure 1-1. It needs to measure and assess itself on all parameters of the model even though its hierarchy of goals—the level-by-level development of PG—is limited only to increasing quantity. The first level could be Improshare® (improved productivity through sharing) with no employee involvement. (See Chapters 3, 5, and Glossary.) Each successive level is denoted by ever-increasing employee involvement and total financial integration of the PG reward system. It is perfectly plausible for firms to start at their appropriate level and evolve to some higher state in the hierarchy of PG goals.

The management of this hypothetical firm might believe that making no other changes in the status quo but quantity renders full assessment of the theoretical model unrealistic. This is not the case. The actual weights for each variable will be different (i.e., a different profile), but the choice of limited goals does not negate assessing the full model. To do so would be to ignore any explanation in changes in other variables of productivity such as turnover, quality of work produced, flexibility of the workforce, and dissatisfaction. Failure to achieve even a modest form of PG might be indicated by full assessment of the model. Conversely, success should be easier to achieve by focusing on deficiency areas of the optimal profile for each hierarchical level of PG.

What is the optimal profile for this small manufacturer? First of all, there are no norms in this area. Even if there were, many managers would be reluctant to base their decisions on the experiences of others. Right? It always seems that way at first, but managers do rely on norms developed elsewhere. If they exist, PG-oriented firms will use them. Until they do, a model of critical variables will suffice if management is willing to do its homework and honestly plot its perceived actual profile on a graph and then specify their ideal profile. The ideal profile is the one obtainable over a reasonable time frame, such as one to three years. The ideal requires full understanding of the hierarchy of PG goals and the interplay of the firm's actual profile. We believe that there is a step function explaining the association between optimality and PG success/failure (see Figure 1-2).

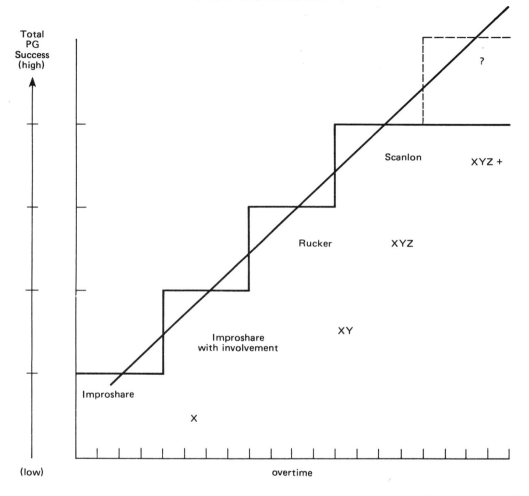

FIGURE 1-2 Hierarchical Productivity Gainsharing Development

Thus, this manufacturing firm might assess its profile by managerial consensus. Actual versus ideal scores can be developed for each of the variables in the model as constrained by organizational goals. Even the degree of consensus, or lack thereof, between managers of this firm will be an interesting finding. This technique is similar to those of organizational development but focuses specifically on PG.

The step functions of Figure 1-2 are explained by the hierarchical development of the organization in interaction with PG. For instance, the first step of PG could be Improshare. The assessment of the macrovariables against our manufacturing firm can be understood by reviewing Table 1-1.

In column one, we have given Improshare with no involvement

9

TABLE 1-1 The Productivity Gainsharing Goal Profile

	IMPROSHARE PLAN		RUCKER PLAN	SCANLON PLAN
	No Involvement	Low Involvement	Medium Involvement	High Involvement
Variables	(Goal–Actual=Δ)	(Goal–Actual=Δ)	(Goal–Actual=Δ)	(Goal–Actual=Δ)
Organizational				
Climate	G – A = Δ	G – A = Δ	G – A = Δ	G – A = Δ
Size	G – A = Δ	G – A = Δ	G – A = Δ	G – A = Δ
Technology	G – A = Δ	G – A = Δ	G – A = Δ	G – A = Δ
Policy	G – A = Δ	G – A = Δ	G – A = Δ	G – A = Δ
Reward Structure	G – A = Δ	G – A = Δ	G – A = Δ	G – A = Δ
Identity	G – A = Δ	G – A = Δ	G – A = Δ	G – A = Δ
Socio-Cultural-Institutional				
Union and Industrial Relations	G – A = Δ	G – A = Δ	G – A = Δ	G – A = Δ
Workforce Characteristics	G – A = Δ	G – A = Δ	G – A = Δ	G – A = Δ
External Environment	G – A = Δ	G – A = Δ	G – A = Δ	G – A = Δ
Individual Level				
Managerial Attitude & Philosophy	G – A = Δ	G – A = Δ	G – A = Δ	G – A = Δ
Trust	G – A = Δ	G – A = Δ	G – A = Δ	G – A = Δ
Locus of Control	G – A = Δ	G – A = Δ	G – A = Δ	G – A = Δ
Aptitude	G – A = Δ	G – A = Δ	G – A = Δ	G – A = Δ
Motivation	G – A = Δ	G – A = Δ	G – A = Δ	G – A = Δ
Satisfaction	G – A = Δ	G – A = Δ	G – A = Δ	G – A = Δ
Financial Variables				
Internal System Attributes	G – A = Δ	G – A = Δ	G – A = Δ	G – A = Δ
External System Attributes	G – A = Δ	G – A = Δ	G – A = Δ	G – A = Δ
	ΣΔX	ΣΔX	ΣΔX	ΣΔX

Scale:
0 — No influence
1-2 — Low influence
3-4 — Moderate influence
5-7 — Medium influence
8-9 — High influence
10 — Total influence (knockout factor)

system optimal goals. Let us assume an assessment of a firm (perhaps by managerial consensus). Given perceived actual scores for the variables of the model, then the scores can be inserted in columns for each type of plan; i.e., the same score is inserted four times. Then, the actual column is to be subtracted from the goal column to produce the difference. This value (+ or – 1) is placed in the difference column (Δ). The sum of the differences (ignore + or – signs and use the whole number) is the degree of deviation from ideal or goal conditions of the profile associated with a particular PG plan.

For our manufacturing firm we have derived measurements of the 17 variables of our model. The sum of the deviations from goal conditions looks like this:

IMPROSHARE		RUCKER	SCANLON
No	Low	Medium	High
Involvement	Involvement	Involvement	Involvement
$\Sigma \Delta 0$	$\Sigma \Delta 7$	$\Sigma \Delta 15$	$\Sigma \Delta 20$

Assuming good measurement and managerial consensus of the actual variables, then the optimum PG plan for this firm is Improshare with no involvement. The reasoning should be clear because the sum of the differences from ideal conditions is zero while the other plans have varying degrees of discrepancy between actual and ideal profiles. Referring to Figure 1–2 we can see that our firm is at the first step of PG hierarchy. Conditions may be such that they never change. That shouldn't prevent the firm from increasing efficiency while deriving the benefits of improved productivity.

As each firm makes its own assessment, the value of having a theoretical model grows. Research will begin to produce goal profiles that are less normative and more empirical. Norms will be developed. The profile scores will become the standards to aim for. The state of our knowledge is such now that we know that really large discrepancy scores are associated with most PG failure.

We believe that Figure 1–2 graphs this relationship. That is, it is inherently more difficult to produce a successful scanlon plan than a successful Improshare plan with no involvement. For example, managerial attitudes and managerial philosophies can be more autocratic under Improshare with no involvement. Only efficiency is being rewarded — typically by working faster. Conversely, with a high-involvement scanlon plan, the same attitudes and beliefs would totally obviate the success of the plan.

It should be clear that large discrepancy scores are most associated with PG failure. This is in spite of corporate miracle stories where, for instance, a scanlon plan "saved" a company from bankruptcy. While this is always possible, what is often overlooked is that any understanding of their profile score was unknown. Some of these case histories reveal high scores on almost all critical variables of the model, save financial. Thus, the closer a firm is to small changes, the easier it is to put into place the PG plan best associated with the hierarchy of goals. Dramatic turnarounds always make good reading, but PG success more commonly reflects hard work and degree of fit between actual conditions and ideal PG variables.

The Notion of Degree of Fit and PG

Since we don't have norms for the profile a given type of firm or a given industry should have, the best strategy appears to prepare management with information and develop baseline measures of the theoretical model. Then, idealized measures can be collected and discrepancy values computed. Mapping where the firm is by measuring its profile allows for selecting the PG plan that requires the least disruption, i.e., fits best. Learning and generalization of PG is incremental and not overly dramatic. When one looks at the literature of PG (Chapter 2), it is clear that the most successful PG firms evolve gradually into their ultra-PG plans. Continuity of dedication and effort is clear and phases of development are usually noted along the parameters of the model.

What support do we have that (1) these model variables are critical and (2) the notion of degree of fit works best?

This book offers a variety of examples of success and failure with PG. Obviously there are many factors associated with either success or failure, but there are observable patterns. The literature-review section denotes how variables A2 (size), A3 (technology), A5 (reward structure), B1 (union and industrial relations), C2 (trust), C5 (motivation), C6 (satisfaction), and D1 (internal system) have all been associated with success and failure. Other chapters go more deeply into variables and their explanatory value in the model. Also, the experience of other experts reflected in Chapters 2, 5, 6, 8, and 9 provides insight into the importance and relative weight of the variables that influence PG. We believe that incremental organizational changes or degree of fit of PG have the best chance for long-range success. One strong reason is that no one form of PG is totally incompatible with another. That is, PG can be viewed on a developmental continuum from low involvement/formula simplicity to high involvement/formula complexity.

Assessment

We have simplified our discussion of the macrovariables so that a tedious exercise in business research is not the reader's first task. However, microvariables actually elicit the measurements of the macrovariables. A casual understanding of business research will indicate that some microvariables are measurable with standard scales, i.e., those used in other research with demonstrated validity and reliability. Other microvariables, such as policy, are believed by experts to be important and are more difficult to measure. However, policy can be measured by the extent of rules, the number of issued SOPs (Standard Operating Procedures), and the perceived constraint of rules.

In spite of our concern to make things simple, management must have confidence in data-based decision making. This includes data that are attitudinal and subjective. With this conviction, management can profile the firm for PG consideration.

Our suggested strategy is to review the PG model in a detailed form, perhaps with consultants. At the same time, the organization may process relevant information on various forms of PG. Then, a task force in charge of the feasibility study must pursue the optimality of PG as per Table 1-1.

The purpose of organizational assessment is to clearly understand managerial philosophies and discuss perceptual differences of organizational goals and the means to accomplish these goals. If this step proves fruitful, then initial assessment for PG profiling appears useful. This assessment will be based on the PG Model and in itself will provide useful data.

Let's assume that some insight exists into the hierarchy of PG goals wished for by management. Decision makers would be left with a series of tables, somewhat like Table 1-1. For the moment, assume perfect theory, excellent cooperation, and valid results. We are still left with scores that show the actual subtracted from the ideal, i.e., the difference score. Remembering Table 1-1, the task force would now like to accept or reject PG, and if it accepts, choose the optimal PG. Since the difference scores are relative to the firm, only the ideal scores of experts can give a clue on how to interpret the difference scores. After all, we indicated that there are no norms with which to contrast the data. Obviously, a first set of data could be compared to later data if these measures are repeated every year. Since many firms take years to select a form of PG, this assessment strategy would help in that process.

Of the five phases of PG assessment indicated in Figure 1-3, each is followed by the opportunity to reject. It may be the case that influential members of the organization ignore the indications of the PG Model. This can happen if, for example, the chief executive officer sees the value in PG without being aware of the discrepancies of goal conditions. Honest disagreements can cause a firm to go to the next phase. Fully understanding that rejection of any or all PG is possible at any stage of assessment will not mitigate commitment. A contingency approach to PG is wisest. Managers, being averse to risks, are often oversold by consultants and academicians who have seen the benefits of PG.

It is time for educated managers to act responsibly by applying a comprehensive model to their situation in a fashion no different from that

FIGURE 1-3 Phases of Productivity Gainsharing Assessment

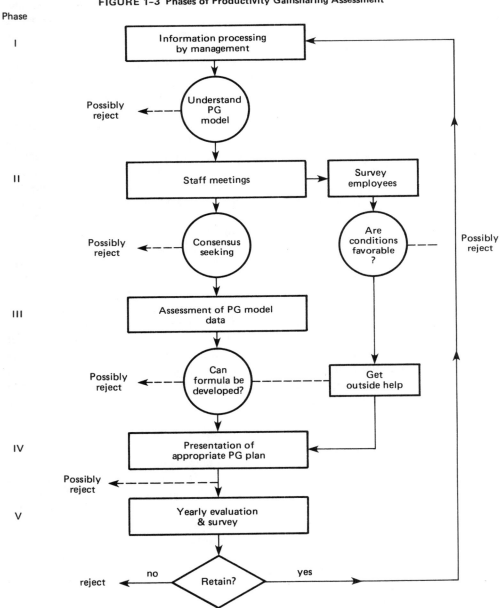

of a cost/benefit analysis. That is, capturing baseline measurements of the PG Model and acting within a consensus of organizational objectives will encourage decision makers to reject PG when it is not indicated as beneficial. Conversely, this same framework for decision making may encourage upgrading PG to the next hierarchical level.

Lastly, as we've clearly indicated in Figure 1-2, the stages in the hierarchy are evolutionary. The dotted lines of the last stage suggest that we do not know the shape and substance of the next higher level of PG. As the readings in this book will show, there are new directions in store for PG—especially as PG transfers from its historical base in manufacturing industries to service and construction industries.

SUMMARY AND CONCLUSION

We began with a review lamenting a theoretical model for PG. Our concern was for creating a data base that could be used for predictive decision making for one firm as well as a comparative data base for many firms. After all, wage and salary surveys serve industry in a similar fashion because empirical job analysis makes valid comparisons possible.

A theoretical model of PG was introduced on two axes: (1) productivity and (2) time. Macro-level variables were described, and their interrelationships to the PG model were explained. Scaling an organization on this PG model produces a set of diagnostic profiles. Discussion elaborated how the model might work in practice.

The dilemma of what a profile means, how to use the profile for decision making, and the notion of degree of fit for PG were explored. We probably raised questions at a time when the reader was looking for answers. Nevertheless, we defend the choice of these variables throughout this book. Also, most research to date as well as expert judgment supports the variables of the model.

Finally, we introduced the reader to the process of assessment. It is a multistage process that follows the ideas presented in this section. In addition, we finished our discussion with a reprise of the difficulties of absolute versus relative measures in diagnostic profile. We chose to be optimistic in the role of the scientific method for business research. Specifically, a framework for organizational change via PG requires a systematic approach. If that framework includes important variables measured by standard methods, the cumulative effect is knowledge for the firm. By building on these data, research efforts can be aggregated to prove out the PG model for a large number of related situations.

2

The Literature of PG

by Brian E. Graham-Moore

National interest in productivity gainsharing has increased in recent years due to our declining levels of productivity. The American experience with PG, however, might have begun with the Nunn-Bush Shoe Company of Milwaukee on July 2, 1935. Another firm was involved in organization-wide productivity gainsharing near that time, but published records are few.[1]

The name Joseph Scanlon immediately surfaces during this period. A former cost accountant, steelworker, union official, and, finally, lecturer at the Massachusetts Institute of Technology, Scanlon has been so important to the productivity gainsharing movement that it was suggested that a generic term for productivity gainsharing (hereafter PG) be the scanlon plan.[2] Scanlon himself never suggested this idea, but his support of PG had a strong influence on a generation of managers, labor leaders, consultants, and academicians. These individuals have kept PG alive to this day, even to the point of institutionalizing it in the Scanlon Plan Association.

This chapter organizes the literature covering PG in order to present an overview of the field. The scanlon plan has received so much attention in the PG literature that other contributions are often overshadowed. Of particular interest is one of the newest and most successful forms of PG—named Improshare.® It may prove to have more impact in 5 years than scanlon plans have had in 40.

16

WHAT IS PRODUCTIVITY GAINSHARING?

PG involves a measurement of productivity combined with a calculation that offers a mutual stake in the sharing of any increases to total organizational productivity, usually with all those responsible for the increases. Total productivity is an all-encompassing term when we consider that outside forces also affect a firm's productivity. Also, the lack of financial productivity can eliminate the gains of performance productivity.

Productivity has been defined by most economists as output per hour of all persons. As this ratio of output to input increases, real economic growth occurs. With such a broad definition, there are many factors that influence productivity, not the least of which could be technology, quality of the workforce, and capital investments. Many forces can influence these factors.

Therefore, an understanding of aggregate economic behavior does not always apply to specific firm-level behavior. Each firm must study its own economic behavior before accepting the economic central tendencies of a nation or an industry. For example, the relationship between sales value of production and the labor cost it takes to produce the product can be remarkably stable for many industries.[3,4] Any company can refer to the U.S. Department of Commerce for reports on its industry's average value added per $1.00 of plant payroll. It is estimated by the Eddy-Rucker-Nickels Company, a consulting firm, that 9 out of 10 manufacturers demonstrate these stable co-variations between sales value of production and labor cost.[5] However, any specific firm must ask itself, What is our past average productivity level?

Of the many variables that go into measuring total productivity, one significant variable is labor productivity. Thus, PG is best understood when described as labor productivity gainsharing. Although nonlabor factors influence labor costs, a firm probably will base its sharing with employees of gains in productivity out of the decrease in expected labor cost. Therefore, PG might also be labeled "expected" labor productivity gainsharing.

Whether Improshare or not, all PG plans require that a historical standard of expected labor costs be computed. Any increase in output combined with the same or lower actual labor cost creates a bonus. Most PG plans split this bonus between the company and the total workforce.[6] The mechanics of establishing the historical standard are not necessarily simple. How to construct the bonus payout denotes the variant of PG—be it Improshare, Rucker, or a scanlon plan. However, the keys to all successful PG formulas are

1. that the normal, average, or standard labor cost is measurable;
2. that the ratio of either sales value of production or units of production value to labor cost is relatively stable; and

17

3. that the policy established for sharing true increases in labor productivity is fair.[7]

PG formulas that meet the objectives above should be able to produce motivating bonuses. In fact, this statement can be validated retrospectively with data from the firm's own experience. PG formulas can be calculated with historical accounting data. Bonus calculations can be modeled, and management can ask itself, What if we had a bonus (that week or month)? Would there have been greater gains? Would productivity have gone higher? Would quality improve, turnover and absenteeism decrease? Would we, as managers, have had more flexibility to achieve improved methods, or, perhaps, greater volume to exploit our markets? The answers to these questions are derived from the combined judgment of management. Given a 5% to 25% bonus, it ought to know if the workforce would increase productive behavior.

Complete answers to the questions above require introduction of the rest of the description of PG—the behavioral and philosophical elements. Here, the literature has been extensive. One of the best sources is Frost, Wakely, and Ruh.[8] Dr. Carl Frost capped many years of successful scanlon experience in collaborating on this book. Comprehensive exposition into the philosophy of scanlonism is undertaken. For example, they delineate what they call the three conditions for a scanlon plan. Basically, the conditions refer to identity, participation, and equity.

By identity, Frost and his associates mean a clear statement of organizational goals and intended achievements. Furthermore, this identity of organizational goals and intended achievements should meld with personal goals that each employee would like to achieve via his or her role in the organization. If organizational and personal goals are one, then the instrument to make both happen is the congruence or the perceived identity of both. While the organization can strive to communicate its objectives, clarifying how the individual matches personal goals with these objectives is a constant educational process.

The second condition is participation. Frost and his associates quite simply assert that participation is the opportunity provided to the employee to be involved while exercising responsibility. Increasing the employee's awareness of his or her responsibility for achieving a fiscally sound and competitive organization is essential if both the employee and firm are to fulfill themselves. Clearly, increased participation reinforces individual commitment to and identification with the firm.

The third condition is the mutual commitment to equity—by employee and the firm. In effect, the firm strives to create a return to all employees for their participation and increased responsibility. This return is financially based in the PG formula. Thus, the investment of all employees in identity and participation is enhanced by a fair method for sharing increases to productivity. Interest in the firm, reliable performance, and mutual trust are exchanged for an equitable formula for sharing.

Initial interest in PG often focuses on the formula, the payout, or the bonus because managers do not want to create a giveaway. Once the exercise of researching, constructing, and testing a PG formula is completed, however, it becomes apparent that most formulas will work. Then, the philosophical and behavioral differences associated with the varying PG formulas need careful understanding as they become more important. It is for this reason that the Frost book is so useful, as it delves into these issues more than any other source. To aid in the description of the calculations, however, we will look at four generic types of PG plans: (1) scanlon-simple, (2) scanlon-complex, (3) Rucker, and (4) Improshare.

Scanlon Calculation—Simple

The original scanlon plan is attributed to Joseph Scanlon's assistance in helping save the Empire Steel and Tin Plate Company. President of his union local and trained in cost accounting, Scanlon was convinced that his own union's demands would force the company into bankruptcy. Through his leadership, management and labor made a strong effort to improve labor-management cooperation. Scanlon believed that the average worker was a great reservoir of untapped information concerning labor-saving methods. Workers needed a mechanism permitting them "to work smarter, not harder." This following excerpt epitomizes Joe Scanlon's belief in labor-management cooperation:

> One of the greatest advantages of this kind of collective bargaining from the worker's point of view, is the knowledge that it gives him of the business. When a slump is coming, he knows it. He is even given a chance to combat it, in the sense that if he can devise a cheaper way of turning out his product, perhaps the company will be able to take away business from somebody else. In a number of instances the Lapointe workers have actually done this, the most spectacular example being that of an order from a big automotive concern in December, 1942. The workers had been pressing management to accept orders even at the break-even point so as to tide over a bad period. Mr. Prindiville, who sometimes sits in on the screening-committee meetings, had given in to the pressure some months previously to the extent of taking an order from this firm for 100 broaches at $83 per broach. But Lapointe had lost 10 percent on the deal, and Mr. Prindiville now put his foot down. If this business was to be taken again the price would have to be raised. In view of new competition, it meant that Lapointe almost certainly would not get the business—at a time when work was scarce. The gloomy gathering that listened to Mr. Prindiville's pronouncement was then electrified

by a question from Jimmie McQuade, skilled grinder and one of the most outspoken members of the screening committee. Who says we can't make those broaches at that price for a profit? Mr. McQuade wanted to know. If you'd give the men in the shop a chance to go over the blueprints before production starts and to help plan the job, there are lots of ways of cutting costs without cutting quality. The idea grew, and the next day the suggestion ran around the shop like wildfire. The order was taken at the old price, this time with a profit of 10 percent—a total gain in efficiency of 20 percent. The truth is that the Scanlon Plan has generated a competitive spirit throughout the factory: one hears as much about competition from the workers as from management itself. If there is a question of struggling for existence the whole company struggles collectively, and all the brains available are focused on the fight. The worker is no longer a pawn in a game he does not understand. He is a player. He enjoys it. And his contribution is worth money to all concerned.[9]

This kind of story is common to most contemporary scanlon companies. Such companies enjoy a very high degree of employee involvement. In a word, they have teamwork. One measure of this involvement is the high percentage of suggestions received and put into use.[10, 11]

While sentiments about cooperation, participation, teamwork, and unleashing the knowledge of the worker depicted the original scanlon plan, the first plan had no bonus calculation.[12] Joe Scanlon ultimately designed a bonus system to reinforce these philosophies. By that time he was working for the production-engineering department of United Steel Workers. The Adamson Company in East Palestine, Ohio, was the first company to try a bonus calculation constructed by Joe Scanlon. In many ways, this calculation is the most imitated—at least in principle. The most commonly applied formula is generalized as:

$$\text{Base ratio} = \frac{\text{Labor costs}}{\text{Sales value of production}}$$

Scanlon's idea was to focus the attention of everyone on those variables within the control of the firm and its human resources. The apparent simplicity of the calculation placed it quickly into use. At the same time, the scanlon plan became the darling of the industrial relations literature focusing on labor-management cooperation. Most industrial relations personnel textbooks include a section on this scanlon plan. But in terms of the bonus calculation, there is no one scanlon plan.[13]

Scanlon Calculations—Complex

One of the causes of scanlon plan failure has been attributed to the formula.[14] In almost all instances these were simple scanlon formulas, i.e., the single ratio. Product mix has been cited as a problem for the simple ratio to capture. Firms with many product lines that vary in labor content, such as produced labor or buy-out labor, were either overcalculating or under-calculating the expected labor cost. Thus, the split ratio formula grew out of necessity. Controllers developed a base ratio for each product line, which could more accurately reflect a fair measure of labor input.[15] The split ratio formula deals more equitably with problems of product mix. A single ratio formula mentioned in Chapter 3, for example, overpays by $40,000 when there is no true increase in productivity. The allowed labor formula, another scanlon-type calculation, is discussed extensively in Moore and Ross.[16]

A crucial difference between this calculation and "traditional" scan-lon calculations is that it excludes sales and bases its measurement on direct labor productivity. The rationale is to decrease problems of product mix and variation in selling price. This formula assumes that accounting data or engineered time standards are available for all direct hours. Then, allowed times are based on actual past performance. The allowed hour formula can be seen as antithetical to the scanlon philosophy of team-work and cooperation because it can easily become a management tool. Since allowed labor can be calculated for product line and department, the split ratio calculation could isolate problem areas and corrective action could be taken. Clearly, this is a goal of PG, but only mature PG firms can take advantage of this kind of information—for example, Lincoln Electric.[17]

A more useful, sophisticated formula is the multicost ratio.[18] This formula approaches profit sharing—which, of course, is not technically PG. It is reported, in fact, that many profit-sharing firms are inclined to have other incentives, including PG.[19] Profit-sharing plans take their place alongside Improshare, scanlon, and Rucker plans as alternate or comple-mentary ways to bring about more productivity as well as a mutually beneficial relationship between management and employees.

Except for its timing, profit sharing is the ultimate in the total sys-tem incentive approach because it links motivation and reward to the final measure of corporate performance—i.e., profits.[20] Profit sharing rewards or penalizes all those who contribute to the growth of the enterprise in relation to the firm's "economic productivity"—physical productivity as accepted by and paid for by the market, the only arena where it really counts.

The idea behind the multicost ratio is to include all costs. The base ratio becomes:

$$\text{Base ratio} = \frac{\text{Labor} + \text{all costs}}{\text{Sales value of production}}$$

Assuming a firm has a comprehensive, sophisticated accounting system, this calculation can be made monthly—which, of course, makes its timing better than profit sharing. Now, problems of product mix and inflation reported in case studies of failures[21] are considerably decreased. (The description and proper use of the multicost ratio calculation is explained in Chapter 3.)

It is unlikely that a firm first trying PG should attempt this formula because of the behavioral considerations. The objectives of PG are to involve everyone, at some level, with the overall goal of productivity.[22,23,24] If the complex PG formula is difficult to understand, it might engender distrust, or be perceived as a gimmick. Obviously, acceptance and learning are thwarted. Scanlon formulas, as well as other PG formulas, have been over-simplified in the literature or completely overlooked.

Rucker Plan

Using studies of data collected by the U.S. Census and Surveys of Manufacturers, Allan W. Rucker showed in the early thirties that economic productivity had been extremely stable from 1899 to 1929.[25]A parallel analysis for the years 1964 to 1968 was conducted by P. J. Loftus, Director of the Statistical Office of the United Nations. The results were the same. While each industry has its own pattern, there was a stable relationship between production value and value added by labor.

Publishing in proprietary sources, Rucker performed industry-by-industry analyses of manufacturers. He maintained that 90% of the instances were favorable to PG. Unfortunately, there is a paucity of studies or evaluations on the Rucker Plan. The primary sources are proprietary booklets published by the consultants. Nevertheless, the plan has been successful in a variety of manufacturing firms.

The concept of value added is well known in accounting circles and recently has been the focus of attention for pay systems.[26,27]As with all PG plans, this formula can be tailored to include only workers with a very close connection to the production process or all personnel in an organization. Thus, value added is defined as the difference between the value of production (adjustments) less outside purchases such as materials and supplies.

The following example is offered in Table 2-1. Step 1 reflects the difference between the selling price and price adjustments for seasonality. Step 2 reflects subtractions for outside purchases such as materials, supplies, and energy. Value added is $340,000, or 34% of the selling price. Now, Step 4 applies the historical average of labor value added to the product. This is called the Rucker Standard. In this example, 41.17%, or $140,000, is the allowed (or expected) labor cost. Step 5 shows that the actual labor cost was $120,000. Thus, Step 6 reflects a bonus pool of $20,000. A 50/50 split is a common policy (as in Improshare), and Steps 7 and 8 reflect this. Steps 9 and 10 reflect a policy of a reserve for deficit months (as in the case of many scanlon companies). Since the participating

TABLE 2-1 The Rucker Value-Added Formula

VALUE-ADDED CALCULATION METHOD—MONTH X		
1. Value of production (sales ± various adjustments)		$1,000,000
2. Less Outside purchases (material, supplies, energy)		
Material and supplies	$500,000	
Other outside purchases, nonlabor costs	160,000	660,000
3. Value added (#1 - #2)		340,000
4. Allowed employee costs (from diagnostic historical analysis) #3 × 41.17%)		140,000
5. Actual labor (employee costs)		120,000
6. Bonus pool (#4 - #5)		20,000
7. Company share (50% × #6)		10,000
8. Employee share (#6 - #7)		10,000
9. Reserve for deficit months (20% × #8)		2,000
10. Bonus pool (#8 - #9)		8,000
11. Participating payroll		80,000
12. Bonus percentage (#10 ÷ #11)		10%

Source: B.E. Moore and T.L. Ross, *The Scanlon Way to Improved Productivity* (New York: Wiley-Interscience, 1978) p. 81.

payroll is $80,000 (Step 11), then the bonus percentage becomes 10% in Step 12.[28]

There are many similarities between Rucker and scanlon—and to some extent Improshare. Actually there is no one Rucker Plan. In principle, the different PG plan formulas vary in subtle yet profound ways. Subtle, because the measurements all attempt to capture the ratio of labor inputs to production outputs. Profound, because the sensitivity of the measurements can be magnified by environmental and product mix factors in ways which could be a problem if left unchecked. Lastly, the differences in the formulas can be a behavioral consideration. That is, no PG plan will work without acceptance and some level of trust. With this in mind, it should be remembered that a Rucker Plan can share many similarities with scanlon plans. Much of the information to be reviewed concerning scanlon plans can be generalized by analogy to the Rucker Plan. But again, there is a paucity of evaluation research on the Rucker Plan, even though it has been in existence for over 30 years.

Improshare

Improshare means improved productivity through sharing. It is relatively new to the field of PG. Invented in 1973, it is the creation of Mitchell Fein, an educator, consultant, and industrial engineer. Because of its overall simplicity and lack of emphasis on employee involvement, Improshare is relatively easy to install. The plan focuses on the number of work hours saved for a given number of units produced. The actual hours taken to produce a given number of units are subtracted from hours required (or expected) to produce the same number of units. Savings realized by producing a given number of units in reduced hours are shared by the firm and the worker. There are three key factors to Improshare:

1. work-hour standard;
2. Base Productivity Factor;
3. understanding by most workers of the relationship of hours worked to units produced.

By definition, a work-hour standard is the total production hours worked divided by the units produced. The acceptable standard could be produced by engineered standards (e.g., time studies) or by data based on experience. Either way—or both—it is the norm or expected hours required to produce an acceptable level of output.

The Base Productivity Factor, or BPF, is the total production and nonproduction hours divided by the value of work in work hours. For an example, see Table 2-2.

The third key factor associated with Improshare is the simplicity of the formula and its ready comprehension by the workforce. While Fein has stated that many elements of Improshare's formula have been in use for twenty years,[29] he has assembled a formula that avoids some problems of scanlon-type formulas while offering the concept of productivity to the worker in a psychologically real form. Americans probably think in terms of so many hours to produce so many units of work. Indeed, we are a time-conscious culture.

There is some evidence to suggest that workers in scanlon firms need to understand the bonus formula. Many scanlon firms spend a great deal of time educating the workforce about the formula—often to little avail. Conversely, one study of an Improshare firm shows that line supervisors can readily explain what factors influence the formula to their subordinates.[30]

Fein has incorporated elements of the Halsey premium plan (which dates from 1890) into an organizationwide formula. By pooling all production and nonproduction hours from a selected base period, Fein created the BPF. This is a significant contribution. The BPF, while based on time standards, is a composite measure of productive and nonproductive work. Since there are no standards on nonproductive work, a necessary assumption is that the relationship between productive and nonproductive work is reasonably constant. The BPF, therefore, is constructed with data from an average period of productivity, or one that management recognizes as acceptable. This is different from a scanlon analysis, which looks at the

TABLE 2-2 The Improshare Formula

BASE PERIOD OF ACCEPTABLE PRODUCTIVITY

Facts: 40 direct and 20 indirect employees

$$\text{Work hour standard} = \frac{\text{Total production work hours}}{\text{units produced}}$$

$$\text{Product A} = \frac{20 \text{ employees} \times 40 \text{ hours}}{1000 \text{ pieces}} = 0.8 \text{ per piece or } .8 \times 1000 = 800$$

$$\text{Product B} = \frac{20 \text{ employees} \times 40 \text{ hours}}{500 \text{ pieces}} = 1.6 \text{ per piece or } 1.6 \times 500 = 800$$

Total standard value hours 1,600 in Base Period

$$\text{Base Productivity Factor (BPF)} = \frac{\text{Total production and nonproduction hours}}{\text{Total standard value hours}}$$

$$\text{BPF} = \frac{\begin{array}{c}(40 \text{ direct employees} \times 40 \text{ hours}) \\ + (20 \text{ indirect employees} \times 40 \text{ hours})\end{array}}{\text{actual hours}}$$

$$= \frac{2{,}400 \text{ production hours}}{1{,}600 \text{ standard value hours}} = 1.5$$

BONUS CALCULATION FOR MONTH X

Product A = 0.8 hours × 600 units × 1.5BPF	= 720
Product B = 1.6 hours × 900 units × 1.5BPF	= 2,160
Improshare hours (standard hours for actual units produced)	= 2,880
Less actual hours (assumed)	= 2,280
Gained hours	**600**
	===

$$\text{Employee share} \left(50\% \text{ of } 600 = \frac{300}{2280} = 13.1\% \right)$$

Source: Adapted from *Productivity Sharing Programs: Can They Contribute to Productivity Improvement?* U.S. General Accounting Office, AFMD-81-22, March 3, 1981: 11.

total budget period. Clearly, the emphasis of Improshare is to reinforce quantity. The calculation is constructed to "beat yesterday's performance" if yesterday was a representative day. Once the BPF is computed it "represents the relationship in the base period between actual hours worked by all employees in the group and the value of the work in (work hours) produced by these employees" [p. 481].[31]

The timing for Improshare has been perfect. The acceptance of Improshare has been high—Firestone, Hooker Chemical Company, Rockwell International, Ingersoll-Rand, Prestolite, Atlas Powder Company, McGraw-Edison, and Stanley Home Products, to name but a few, have one or more locations with Improshare working well.

While a series of educators, consultants, managers, and labor leaders have contributed to the development of scanlon-type plans, Mitchell Fein is unique in his singular contribution to PG. The following is an excerpt from "An Alternative to Traditional Managing."

> Traditional work measurement established the time it "should take" to perform a given task under prescribed conditions, not how long it took to perform the work in the past. Such normal or fair day's work standards are established through performance rating with stop watch time study or predetermined standards, against a defined measurement base. This leveling or normalizing of observed data is the keystone of traditional work measurement; it must be employed.
>
> The arguments that arise in setting traditional time standards are avoided by measuring productivity against the average level of an agreed base period. Using a method called measurement by parameters, standards are set at the average of the past, using historical data within a place of work, with no need to performance rate the work performance data. The rationale for this approach is that "yesterday's" performance is established as the Accepted Productivity Level (AFL). Measurements in the future will be made against this APL base [p. 481].[32]

Traditional work measurement may seem antithetical to some of the assumptions of PG—namely, it might remind one of the individual incentives. Yet, a measure of labor productivity must start somewhere. Fein has blended many older ingredients into a newer, successful package. However, there is no set philosophy associated with Improshare.

Mentioned earlier, for example, was the fact that no employee involvement is required to install Improshare. Technically this is true, but in practice Improshare may have almost the same advance build-up as a scanlon plan, including the installation of a suggestion system. That is, an outside consultant may prepare management with a program and training so that employees have sufficient information about the plan. However, there is no particular structure to Improshare as there is with scanlon. Fein favors good communications and believes that labor-management committees under scanlon plans are too structured [p. 41].[33]

In point of fact, Improshare can be installed in either autocratic or participative management firms. Labor-management committees, suggestion systems, and other examples of employee involvement may or may not be a part of Improshare. PG exists in many forms and can become a way of life in any of them. For example, Lincoln Electric has the nation's most successful incentive system and there is no commitment to a sophisticated management philosophy. Instead, Lincoln strives to maximize every day in every way the shared gains in increased productivity. There are only two known in-depth publications about Lincoln Electric,[34,35] and the inference to be drawn from these works is that personnel of Lincoln Electric are highly motivated by extrinsic rewards and have a highly rational view towards productivity.

In many ways, Improshare spans the gap between those firms with no interest in participative management and concepts such as the quality of work, and those firms that do expose those management philosophies. Therefore, Improshare is, above all, a formula which can be applied to many situations. As a formula, however, Fein argues it is a "way of life" because management obligates itself to a set of rules, yet places no limitations on the workers.[36] No memo of understanding, vote, or commitment is sought in advance from the employees. The purpose of Improshare is to make workers "bottom-line oriented."

PG INVOLVEMENT

While other PG plans may or may not have a structure to achieve labor-management cooperation and participation, all known scanlon organizations have a commitment to a highly structured suggestion system that involves much involvement. Predating Quality Control Circles, scanlon committees strive to produce productivity-related suggestions. This aspect of scanlonism has been generally impressive.

Moore (see Chapter 4) has analyzed suggestion-making at DeSoto, Inc. of Garland, Texas. The pattern of results at DeSoto is similar to many other scanlon companies. DeSoto's experience indicates that most employees find quantity-improving suggestions easiest to make. Quality and cost-reduction suggestions lag considerably.

Ideally, nonproductivity-related suggestions should disappear after the first year of scanlon experience. Apparently, this channel of communication, once opened, will always incur some suggestions motivated by irritation within the organization. Since the involvement system is not by definition a grievance procedure, these suggestions normally are referred to the appropriate channels by most firms.

Two critiques of the involvement system are a part of the literature. Gray[37] maintains that in a large English automobile body-stamping plant, production committees used more work hours than was cost effective. Fein, speaking for Improshare, favors labor-management committees or Quality Control Circles and believes scanlon committees are "too structured."[38]

One fact is irrefutable. Scanlon production and screening committees produce more accepted and implemented suggestions than are produced by individual suggestion systems. Typically, the percentage of employees who make (or co-author) at least one suggestion a year ranges from 46% to 95% of all employees in scanlon companies. In individual suggestion systems only 26% of the total workforce makes at least one suggestion a year.[39] By rotating personnel through the scanlon committee system, workers are brought into close contact with management while both pursue problem solving. Scanlon managers clearly identify with participative management philosophies.[40,41] The structure of the involvement system makes new assignments routine, and guarantees representation of employees. (See chapter 4.) Mature scanlon companies have had virtually all employees serving at some time in the committee system. Peer review of suggestions makes reinforcement of suggestion-making behavior easier—whether accepted or rejected.[42] The scanlon involvement system is a form of organization development as it becomes a new communication structure for many firms.[43,44] Most literature on the scanlon plan cites not only participation and communication but also willingness, cooperation, and acceptance of change that occur because of the structure and process of the suggestion system.[45,46,47,48,49,50]

For years, the only evaluation studies of scanlon plans came from MIT, due to its historical connection with Joe Scanlon and, later, Frederick Lesieur. In the midwest, Dr. Carl Frost has been directly responsible for the direction and leadership of the Scanlon Plan Association, based at Michigan State University. This association has had considerable impact on firms generally in Michigan, Ohio, Indiana, and Illinois. Occasional studies lead to published reports but almost exclusively for its own membership.

In general, this is the type of evidence modern managers wish to see. Older literature is replete with testimonials and anecdotes. Today's decision makers and behavioral scientists want more quantitative information and they want it collected rigorously within a theoretical framework. In spite of this, case studies have been the predominant method of scanlon and PG study until the late 1960s. It is possible to review older case studies and newer empirical studies by organizing them around their principle findings—regardless of their methodology. The following are organizational or environmental conditions associated with scanlon plan research:

- Front-line supervisors may feel threatened by the suggestion system because they feel they are no longer bosses or because a high rate of suggestions makes their past behavior look autocratic.[51,52,53]
- The performance norm is difficult to adjust in the face of changing conditions.[54,55,56]
- A fair measurement of an organization's performance may be impossible.[57,58]
- Managerial attitudes must either favor participative management or be disposed to change.[59,60]
- Previous wage structures, such as individual incentive-suggestion systems, must be phased out. Compromises here are common and lead to transitional (protected) rates.[61,62,63]
- The plan can focus too intently on labor savings while not providing sufficient attention to other sources of savings.[64]

- The characteristics of the firm, such as size, management philosophy, climate, technology, sophistication of accounting systems require matching PG to optimize on these factors.[65,66,67]

Lawler devotes a chapter to PG in *Pay and Organizational Development*.[68] His review of the PG literature is summarized in Table 2-3.

Now that Improshare is so popular, we may begin to see evaluation studies of its outcomes. A reported 100 companies have experimented

TABLE 2-3   Conditions Favoring Gainsharing Plans

ORGANIZATIONAL CHARACTERISTIC	FAVORABLE CONDITION
Size	Small unit, usually fewer than 500 employees
Age	Old enough so that learning curve has flattened and standards can be set based on performance history
Financial measures	Simple, with a good history
Market for output	Good, can absorb additional production
Product costs	Controllable by employees
Organizational climate	Open, high level of trust
Style of management	Participative
Union status	No union, or one that is favorable to a cooperative effort
Overtime history	Limited to no use of overtime in past
Seasonal nature of business	Relatively stable across time
Work floor interdependence	High to moderate interdependence
Capital investment plans	Little investment planned
Product stability	Few product changes
Comptroller/Chief financial officer	Trusted, able to explain financial measures
Communication policy	Open, willing to share financial results
Plant manager	Trusted, committed to plan, able to articulate goals and ideals of plan
Management	Technically competent, supportive of participative management style, good communications skills, able to deal with suggestions and new ideas
Corporate position (if part of larger organization)	Favorable to plan
Workforce	Technically knowledgeable, interested in participation and higher pay, financially knowledgeable and/or interested
Plant support services	Maintenance and engineering groups competent, willing, and able to respond to increased demands

Source: E.E. Lawler, *Pay and Organizational Development,* Reading, Mass: Addison-Wesley, 1981.

with or installed Improshare. (See Chapter 5.) By analogy, some of the scanlon findings on outcomes may be replicated in evaluation studies of Improshare and other forms of PG—if they emulate the philosophy of scanlonism.

The literature of PG, until recently, has been focused on the scanlon plan. Key issues are delineated below and supporting studies are cited.

- The plan enhances coordination, teamwork, and sharing knowledge at lower levels.[69,70,71,72,73,74]
- Social needs are recognized via participation and mutually reinforcing group behavior.[75,76,77]
- Attention is focused on cost savings—not just quantity.[78,79]
- Acceptance of change due to technology, market, and new methods is greater since higher efficiency leads to bonus.[80,81]
- Attitudinal change of workers occurs and they demand more efficient management and better planning.[82]
- Workers try to reduce overtime; to work smarter, not harder or faster.[83,84,85]
- Workers produce ideas as well as effort.[86,87,88]
- More flexible administration of union-management relationship occurs, including rationale of competence.[89]

IS SIZE A FACTOR?

A factor common to PG success seems to be the employment level of a company (the range is from 80 to 6,000 individuals). While this fact of the relationship of organizational size to PG success is disputed,[90,91] the median employment of scanlon companies is 250 employees.[92,93] There appears to be a point at which organizationwide incentives lose their impact. Larger groups find greater difficulty in seeing the relationship between their performance and their reward.[94] White[95] reports, however, no relationship between PG success and company size in the scanlon firms he studied (some 23 firms).

COMMON SOURCES OF PG FAILURES

The most common causes were economic, i.e., wage inequities or no bonuses being possible. Also, the formulas did not adequately reflect rapid changes in product mix. Those studies noting failures are Gilson and Lefcowitz,[96] Gray,[97] Helfgott,[98] Johnson,[99] Jehring,[100] and Ruh et al.[101,102] Gilson and Lefcowitz report poor plan installation, poor understanding of the formula, and a high component of secondary wage earners who preferred individual incentives. Most compelling is the fact that the product mix greatly affected the ratio of the formula. More complex and exhaustive methods of formula construction are now in use.[103] Gray reports large inequities in pay between departments of an English auto body manufacturer. In this case, as with other plan failures, the formula did not adequately reflect rapid changes in product mix. The results were usually no bonus or bonuses paid with no increase in true productivity. Work practices apparently conflicted with the need for reassigning workers. Conflict rather than cooperation ensued. Gray indicated that "bonuses were inadequate (and) disillusionment with participation appeared. . . ."[p. 242].[104] Gray challenged the motivational role of the suggestion system. That is, he believed that if the suggestion system is to be learned as an instrumental way to increase productivity, why wouldn't it work without a bonus? In another case study, however, Lesieur cites workers actually searching for ways to improve business (by suggestion making) during hard times with no bonuses.[105] Then, too, management attitudes can greatly affect the commitment to PG. In Jehring's study management decided to shift its emphasis to a profit-sharing plan when keeping the PG formula accurate was perceived as too difficult.

PG AS A WAY OF LIFE

PG can become a way of life. A firm successfully embarking on the route to PG begins a form of organization development. One of the driving forces of PG is to unleash the intelligence of the worker.[106,107] It is not surprising that a Firestone manager with experience with Improshare states, "No one knows the job better than the one doing it."[108]

Given that a job incumbent knows his or her job better than anyone else, just how does a firm unleash this knowledge? The variables of Chapter 1 come quickly to mind because involvement, trust, and managerial philosophy become crucial. Does this firm have optimal levels of these variables so that individual growth will become congruent with organizational objectives? Within the framework of a scanlon-like involvement system, many of the steps of a scanlon trial year are analogous to the steps of organizational development (OD).

French and Bell[109] have listed eight common steps or factors of the OD structure and process. Table 2-4 starts with step 1, diagnostic activities. This step frequently includes measurement of opinions and attitudes in order to find out where the organization is. Frequently, scanlon-like PG trial years use the same approach in order to gauge whether to begin or to develop a base-line measure with which to compare growth. Interestingly, problem identification for OD refers to process consulting wherein basic learning situations are presented to clarify perception and under-

TABLE 2-4 Organization Development Activities and Scanlon Counterparts

1. Diagnostic activities: attitude and opinion measurement, including formal measurement that comprises formal questionnaires or interviewing to ascertain the state of the organization	1. Trial year evaluation measurements
2. Problem identification: process consulting to help perception and understanding of individual, group, and organizational-level issues	2. At all times in the involvement system
3. Goal setting and methods achievement: planning, utilizing information from problem solving, and to compare the real versus the ideal	3. Management's direction, especially through the screening committee and through the influence of the formula
4. Communication improvement: survey feedback activities, education and training activities, to improve coordination	4. All committees improve this, plus annual questionnaire will help
5. Conflict identification and resolution: third-party peacemaking, confrontation counseling to improve cooperation	5. Peer review of suggestions in production committees is a form of open problem solving
6. Task forces: team building intergroup activities to enhance cooperation	6. Group suggestion making is a very common outcome of the plan
7. Job design: technostructural activities to improve technical or structural aspects of work	7. One of the most common outcomes of scanlon plans is acceptance of technical change
8. Measurement and evaluation: assessment activities to produce information on "where we are"	8. Annual survey, financial analysis, and annual scanlon meeting

Source: B.E. Moore and T.L. Ross, *The Scanlon Way to Improved Productivity* (New York: Wiley-Interscience, 1978), p. 151.

standing. These learning situations are usually handled in special training sessions. Conversely, these opportunities to learn are created within involvement systems. For example, a worker may be a member in a committee to research the usefulness of a suggestion. The particular suggestion may not truly be acceptable, yet the worker will search for ways to make it acceptable through modification and improvement rather than dismissing the suggestion. The result is that the original suggestor, the helping committee member, and management gain a new understanding and respect for one another. The suggestion may be enhanced and accepted. The committee member handles new tasks. Management acquires a new respect for the worker. The firm gains a productivity-related suggestion. None of these experiences happen in a training session. Rather, they are real and not artificial experiences which become part of the human fabric of the firm.

Table 2–4 illustrates many subsequent steps or factors associated with OD and scanlon-like involvement. In each of these factors, the analogue exists in the involvement system. For example, OD Activity 3 (Goal setting and methods achievement) is often an exercise in an OD training exercise, while scanlon firms demonstrate a natural process of good communication through the committee system. OD Activity 4 (Communication) here again is achieved in scanlon firms through the committee system, the give and take of suggestion making and evaluation, and of course, any annual surveys fed back. In sum, most identifiable OD activities are found in scanlon firms.

SUMMARY AND CONCLUSION

This chapter took as its objective to review the PG literature. Other reviews[110,111,112] have focused selectively on the scanlon plan almost to the exclusion of other forms of PG. Most reviews are purely descriptive. This chapter attempts to provide some necessary context to the theoretical model of Chapter 1. All of the calculations were presented, but with an eye toward their historical relevance. More extensive treatments are found in Chapter 3 and elsewhere.[113,114] Rather, this review relates the case- and survey-oriented studies to involvement, size, and, sources of failure.

Most of the early literature depicts "everyman as a capitalist" and focuses on labor management cooperation and participation. Unfortunately, much of that literature is anecdotal. Fortunately, more contemporary research broadens the scope of evaluation to most forms of PG. Methods used to assess PG have become more quantitative. Certain key issues, such as size, involvement, and sources of failure, have been identified. We now know what PG is, what it isn't, and we have a good grasp of what it can realistically do. Perhaps not enough of the literature addresses how PG works and under what circumstances.[115,116] The factors associated with learning reward systems when combined with a developing organization are clearly the more interesting parts of the PG literature since they offer so much promise.

The future of PG as a movement will, in part, be explained by answers to these very basic processes. Finally, the organizational socio-cultural, and financial variables will, in some way, provide a profile associated with varying decisions concerning PG or levels of PG implementation.

NOTES

1. H.L. Nunn, *Partners in Production* (Englewood Cliffs, N.J.: Prentice-Hall, 1961).

2. Brian E. Moore and Timothy L. Ross, *The Scanlon Way to Improved Productivity* (New York: Wiley-Interscience, 1978).

3. P.J. Loftus, "Labor's Share in Manufacturing." *Lloyd's Bank Review* (London), April 1969.

4. Allen W. Rucker, *Labor's Road to Plenty* (Boston: Page, 1937).

5. Carl Heyel, ed. *The Encyclopedia of Management*, 2nd ed. (New York: Van Nostrand Reinhold, 1973).

6. Moore and Ross, *The Scanlon Way*.

7. Ibid., p. 2.

8. Carl F. Frost, J.H. Wakely, and R.A. Ruh, *The Scanlon Plan for Organization Development: Identity, Participation, Equity* (East Lansing: Michigan State University Press, 1974).

9. Frederick G. Lesieur, ed., *The Scanlon Plan: A Frontier in Labor-Management Cooperation* (Cambridge: Technology Press of M.I.T. and New York: John Wiley & Sons, 1958) pp. 249–50.

10. Brian E. Moore, *Sharing the Gains of Productivity* (Scarsdale, New York: Work in America Institute Studies in Productivity, 1982).

11. Brian E. Moore, *A Plant-Wide Productivity Plan in Action: Three Years of Experience with the Scanlon Plan* (Washington, D.C.: National Commission on Productivity and Work Quality, 1975).

12. Carla O'Dell, *Gainsharing: Involvement, Incentives, and Productivity* (New York: American Management Association, 1981).

13. Moore and Ross, *The Scanlon Way*.

14. Moore, *A Plant-Wide Productivity Plan*.

15. Moore and Ross, *The Scanlon Way*.

16. Ibid.

17. James F. Lincoln, *Incentive Management* (Cleveland: Lincoln Electric Company, 1951).

18. Moore and Ross, *The Scanlon Way*.

19. B.L. Metzger, *Profit Sharing in Perspective*, 2nd ed. (Evanston, Ill.: Profit Sharing Research Foundation, 1966).

20. Moore and Ross, *The Scanlon Way*.

21. J.J. Jehring, "A Contrast Between Two Approaches to Total Systems Incentives," *California Management Review*, 1967 (pp. 7–14).

22. Frost, Wakely, and Ruh, *The Scanlon Plan For Organization Development*.

23. Frederick G. Lesieur, ed., *The Scanlon Plan: A Frontier in Labor-Management Cooperation* (Cambridge, Mass.: Technology Press of M.I.T. and New York: John Wiley and Sons, 1958).

24. Moore and Ross, *The Scanlon Way*.

25. Heyel, *Encyclopedia of Management*.

26. G. Copeman, "Wages and Added Value," *Management Today*, June 1977, pp. 45–46.

27. B. Cox, "Formulas for Value Added Incentives," *Accounting* (UK), February 1980, pp. 113–16.

28. Moore and Ross, *The Scanlon Way*.

29. Mitchell Fein, "An Alternative to Traditional Managing," in *Handbook of Industrial Engineering*, ed. Gavriel Salvendy (New York: Wiley, 1981).

30. Ruben S. Alanis and Brian E. Moore, "Organizational Learning of New Incentive Systems: Improshare," (manuscript, The University of Texas at Austin, 1981).

31. Fein, "Alternative to Traditional Managing."

32. Ibid., p. 481.

33. Ibid., p. 41.

34. Lincoln, *Incentive Management*.

35. Robert Zager, "Sharing the Wealth: HRD's Role in Making Incentive Plans Work," *Training*, January 1979, pp. 30–31.

36. Fein, "Alternative to Traditional Managing."

37. R.B. Gray, "The Scanlon Plan—A Case Study," *British Journal of Industrial Relations*, 9, pp. 291–313.

38. Fein, "Alternative to Traditional Managing."

39. Joseph Short and Brian E. Moore, "Preliminary Findings of a Multivariate Analysis of Suggestion Systems Impact on Productivity" (Working Paper, Graduate School of Business, The University of Texas at Austin, 1975).

40. Edward E. Lawler, *Pay and Organization Development* (Reading, Massachusetts: Addison-Wesley, 1981).

41. J.K. White, "The Scanlon Plan: Causes and Correlates of Success," *Academy of Management Journal*, 22 (June 1979): 292–312.

42. Ibid.

43. Lawler, *Pay and Organization Development*.

44. Moore and Ross, *The Scanlon Way*.

45. Lawler, *Pay and Organization Development*.

46. Frederick G. Lesieur and E.S. Puckett, "The Scanlon Plan—Past, Present, and Future" (Proceedings of the 21st Industrial Relations Annual Winter Meeting, 1968) pp. 71–80.

47. Timothy L. Ross and G.M. Jones, "An Approach to Increased Productivity: The Scanlon Plan," *Financial Executive*, February 1972, pp. 23–29.

48. Robert Ruh, J.H. Wakely, and J.C. Morrison, "Education, Ego Need Gratification and Attitudes Toward the Job," (manuscript, East Lansing, Michigan State University, 1972).

49. Joseph N. Scanlon, "Adamson and His Profit-Sharing Plan," Production Series no. 172 (New York: American Management Association, 1947) pp. 10–12.

50. George P. Shultz, "Worker Participation on Production Problems: A Discussion of Experience with the Scanlon Plan," *Personnel*, November 1951, pp. 209–11.

51. Frost, Wakely, and Ruh, *The Scanlon Plan for Organization Development*.

52. Lesieur, *The Scanlon Plan: A Frontier*.

53. William F. Whyte, *Money and Motivation* (New York: Harper and Brothers, 1955).

54. Jehring, "Contrast Between Two Approaches."

55. Robert B. McKersie, "Wage Payment Methods of the Future." *British Journal of Industrial Relations*, June 1963, pp. 191–212.

56. Timothy L. Ross, et al., "Measurement Under the Scanlon Plan and Other Productivity Incentive Plans," (Manuscript, Bowling Green State University, 1975).

57. William J. Howell, Jr., "A New Look at Profit Sharing, Pension and Productivity Plans," *Business Management*, December 1967, pp. 26–42.

58. George Strauss and Leonard R. Sayles, "The Scanlon Plan: Some Organizational Problems," *Human Organization*, Fall 1957, pp. 15–22.

59. Frost, Wakely, and Ruh, *The Scanlon Plan for Organization Development*.

60. Ruh, Wakely, and Morrison, "Education, Ego Need Gratification."

61. T.O. Gilson and M.J. Lefcowitz. "A Plant-Wide Productivity Bonus in a Small Factory—Study of an Unsuccessful Case," *Industrial and Labor Relations Review*, 1957, pp. 284–96.

62. Gray, "The Scanlon Plan—A Case Study."

63. McKersie, "Wage Payment Methods."

64. Ibid.

65. Paul S. Goodman, "The Scanlon Plan: A Need for Conceptual and Empirical Models" (Symposium, 81st Annual Convention, American Psychological Association, 1973).

66. O'Dell, "Gainsharing."

67. White, "The Scanlon Plan: Causes and Correlates of Success."

68. Lawler, *Pay and Organization Development.*

69. Lesieur, *The Scanlon Plan: A Frontier.*

70. McKersie, "Wage Payment Methods."

71. Brian E. Moore and Paul S. Goodman, "Factors Affecting the Impact of a Company-Wide Incentive Program on Productivity" (Final Report submitted to the National Commission on Productivity, 1973).

72. Scanlon, "Adamson."

73. Joseph N. Scanlon, "Remarks on the Scanlon Plan" (Proceedings of the Conference on Productivity, June 4, 1949) pp. 10–14.

74. Sumner H. Slichter, J.J. Healy, and E.R. Livernash, *The Impact of Collective Bargaining on Management* (Washington, D.C.: The Brookings Foundation, 1960).

75. Frost, Wakely, and Ruh, *The Scanlon Plan for Organization Development.*

76. Robert Ruh, R.H. Johnson, and M.P. Scrontino, "The Scanlon Plan, Participation in Decision Making and Job Attitudes," *Journal of Industrial and Organizational Psychology* 1 (1973): 36–45.

77. Whyte, *Money and Motivation.*

78. McKersie, "Wage Payments Methods."

79. Moore and Goodman, "Factors Affecting the Impact."

80. Lesieur, *The Scanlon Plan: A Frontier.*

81. McKersie, "Wage Payment Methods."

82. Lesieur, *The Scanlon Plan: A Frontier.*

83. Ashburn Anderson, "Devising Real Incentives for Productivity," *American Machinist*, June 1978, pp. 115–30.

84. Scanlon, "Adamson."

85. Scanlon, "Remarks."

86. Lesieur, *The Scanlon Plan: A Frontier.*

87. Slichter, Healy, and Livernash, *Impact of Collective Bargaining.*

88. Whyte, *Money and Motivation*.

89. R.B. Helfgott, "Group Wage Incentives: Experience with the Scanlon Plan" (New York: Industrial Relations Counselors, Industrial Relations Memo, 1962).

90. Lesieur, *The Scanlon Plan: A Frontier*.

91. Frederick G. Lesieur and E.S. Puckett, "The Scanlon Plan Has Proved Itself," *Harvard Business Review*, September/October 1969, pp. 109–18.

92. Moore and Goodman, "Factors Affecting the Impact."

93. Shultz, "Worker Participation."

94. H. Campbell, "Group Incentives," *Occupational Psychology*, January 1952, pp. 15–21.

95. White, "The Scanlon Plan: Causes and Correlates of Success."

96. Gilson and Lefcowitz, "Plant-Wide Productivity Bonus."

97. Gray, "The Scanlon Plan: A Case Study."

98. Helfgott, "Group Wage Incentives."

99. R.B. Johnson, "The Scanlon Plan: Criteria for Success in Non-Union Plants" (Master's thesis, School of Industrial Management, M.I.T., 1959).

100. Jehring, "Contrast Between Two Approaches."

101. Robert Ruh, R.L. Wallace, and C.F. Frost, "Management Attitudes and the Scanlon Plan," *Industrial Relations*, 1973, pp. 282–88.

102. Ruh, Johnson, and Scrontino, "The Scanlon Plan, Participation, and Attitudes."

103. Ross et al., "Measurement Under the Scanlon Plan."

104. Gray, "The Scanlon Plan–A Case Study," p. 242.

105. Lesieur, *The Scanlon Plan: A Frontier*.

106. Scanlon, "Adamson."

107. Whyte, *Money and Motivation*.

108. *Hamilton* (Ontario) *Spectator*, November 18, 1980.

109. Wendell L. French and C.H. Bell, *Organization Development: Behavior Science Interventions for Organization Improvement* (Englewood Cliffs, N.J.: Prentice-Hall, 1973).

110. Moore, *A Plant-Wide Productivity Plan*.

111. Moore, *Sharing the Gains of Productivity*.

112. White, "The Scanlon Plan: Causes and Correlates of Success."

113. Moore, *Sharing the Gains of Productivity*.

114. Moore and Ross, *The Scanlon Way*.

115. Goodman, "The Scanlon Plan: Needs for Models."

116. Paul S. Goodman and B.E. Moore, "Factors Affecting Acquisition of Beliefs About a New Reward System," *Human Relations*, June 1976, pp. 571–88.

3

PG Formulas: Developing a Reward Structure to Achieve Organizational Goals

by Max Bazerman and Brian E. Graham-Moore

Perhaps the least understood and most controversial aspect of implementing a productivity gainsharing plan is determining an appropriate formula. This typically causes the most confusion among various groups both inside and outside the focal organization. Management generally seeks to select a formula that is not a giveaway but yet has strong reinforcement properties to increase productivity.

Formula determination can be the leading cause of PG plan disagreement between corporate officials, manufacturing management, personnel, the controller's office, and outside consultants and evaluators. Proper formula determination consists of arriving at a set of complicated judgments in a rational way. The purpose of this chapter is to present a diagnostic tool for organizations to develop the formula that will have the optimal reinforcement properties specified in Chapter 1. We believe that organizations should address all of the issues in this chapter before implementing a PG plan.

THE FIVE-STEP RATIONAL-DECISION APPROACH

Let us begin by outlining a five-step rational-decision approach to the selection of a PG formula. First, an organization should determine the goals it desires to achieve with a PG plan. While all PG organizations claim an interest in improving productivity, a number of other (sub)goals should be specified. For example, does the organization want to encourage smarter work or just harder work? Does the organization think that it is necessary to develop a formula to deal with economic flexibility? Does the organization wish to use the formula as a diagnostic management tool or just as a productivity reinforcer? The organization should specify such goals at the very inception of its PG planning.

The second step in a rational-decision approach to selecting an optimal formula is to identify all of the potential alternative formulas, most of which are discussed in chapter 2. This consists of identifying the existence and implications of all potentially usable formulas.

The third step is to determine the expected consequences of each alternative formula for each of the goals that the organization has specified. Most likely, this step requires a task force of interested parties who discuss the policy implications of each formula.

The fourth step in the rational approach consists of determining the relative importance of the various goals that the organization has specified.

And finally, the fifth step consists of choosing the formula that provides the best fit for the set of goals that the organization hopes to achieve. The purpose of Chapter 1 is to provide the theoretical framework for the evaluation of goals. While this approach sounds almost mechanical, we believe that all organizations need to address each of these steps. Otherwise, the lack of specification of the objectives and expected results can become a primary source of intra-organizational conflict as problems later develop concerning the plan.

Now let us consider a typical approach of implementing a PG plan: Some important individual in the organization hears through the informal network of a way to improve productivity. A renowned consultant is brought in and provides evidence that his or her method has proved empirically to increase productivity. In fact, the consultant can even provide examples where his or her work has been successful in improving productivity. Who can argue with results? The plan is adopted. No consideration was given to the specific goals that the organization wanted to achieve. No serious search was given to alternative PG plans. The probable consequences of the plan could not be evaluated appropriately because the organization never specified what it wanted to achieve. All in all, the organization adopted a plan that may work, but the reason for the selection was probably based on who—which consultant—a few key individuals in the organizations knew, rather than a rational comparative approach as specified above.

This latter method of PG plan implementation typically causes later problems concerning whether the formula is achieving what the organization intended. Since the organization never addressed the issue of goals, different members of the organization have different expectations, and conflict arises. Now, however, reasonable changes in the PG formula are often difficult and costly to implement.

This chapter attempts to address the relevant issues in the selection of a PG formula. Following the approach specified should have the potential to greatly reduce the number of subsequent problems and conflicts many PG organizations experience.

Moore and Ross present the most comprehensive known discussion of (1) formula calculation, (2) alternative formulas, and (3) measurement problems in the context of productivity gainsharing.[1] This chapter does not attempt to reexamine the same issues; rather we attempt to examine a set of issues that build on this previous work. Specifically, this chapter attempts to outline a framework to theoreticians and practitioners that addresses the following issues:

(1) What does the organization expect to gain from a PG formula? (2) How does an organization select among alternative formulas? (3) How do various formulas perform at achieving alternative goals? (4) How does an organization select a formula that will survive in a turbulent environment?

Specifying Goals

Specifying goals sounds like such an obvious step, yet a PG organization so often exhibits symptoms months after formula implementation that suggest that it never clarified the goals of its plan. Nothing is more discouraging than hearing a manufacturing manager say, "I thought the plan would encourage cooperation and that hasn't occurred," when the formula selected by the organization had less potential for reinforcing cooperation than any of the other alternative PG formulas.

This section identifies a series of goals that should be considered. We are not suggesting that all organizations should adopt all the goals listed here and in Chapter 1. Rather, organizations should consciously consider various goals in order to optimize their particular profile of goals.

In addition to specifying decisions that have to be made about goal selection, it is important to note that the process of goal specification is also important. Since a primary idea of PG plans is to provide common goals across an organization, it is important to include all relevant constituencies in the goal specification process. This should include all individuals who will subsequently be needed to implement the plan.

A primary concern in goal setting is clarifying what the organization means when it says it wants to improve productivity. General agreement exists that productivity refers to the ratio of outputs to inputs. However, this can be set into operation in a number of ways. In the most general sense, organizational productivity can be viewed as the comparison of profits (outputs) to investments (inputs). If an organization wants to directly reward this definition of productivity, a profit-sharing system is the most obvious formula. In contrast, in a very specific sense, productivity can be viewed as the amount of manufacturing output produced by a certain amount of direct labor. If an organization wants to reward this definition of productivity, a direct efficiency formula can be implemented. Notice, however, that this type of formula ignores indirect overhead and thus offers no incentive for efficient management. In between these two extremes lies a host of alternative formulas that measure goods produced in comparison to manufacturing labor inputs, both direct and indirect. Although efficient management is now rewarded, line workers may feel that there is a weaker relationship between pay and performance. In addition, since line workers are easier to hire and fire with economic fluctuation than indirect workers, this latter type of formula will be more directly affected by economic fluctuation.

Now, since the various formulas have different behavioral and organizational objectives, it is a good idea for firms to establish baseline measures of where they are in terms of their goals. Once they have accomplished this, they should focus on a rational approach for selecting a formula. All PG formulas can be evaluated against most of the following behavioral and organizational factors:

- strength of reinforcement
- base of cooperation
- scope of the formula
- motivation of harder work
- motivation of smarter work
- motivation of improved methods
- motivation of behavior to produce nonlabor savings
- perceived fairness of formula
- ease of administration
- economic flexibility
- cyclical variation

As indicated in Chapter 1, our purpose is not to support one kind of PG plan or one level of PG development (e.g., only the best possible example). Rather, we are suggesting that a formula can be constructed to best achieve the goals of a firm at whatever baseline state that might be. Goals should require a firm to stretch for them, but should not be so high that they contribute to frustration due to lack of attainment. However, those firms embarking on PG should specify their organizational goals. The firm should view these goals within the theoretical framework suggested in Chapter 1 so that it can select and evaluate a PG formula against the factors discussed here.

One of the very first considerations is for decision makers to specify what they mean by productivity. How extensive will the definition be? Who contributes to productivity? Each PG formula has different impact on the subgoals of productivity. Therefore, PG strategic planning should concern itself with all relevant behavioral and organizational factors within the context of a common understanding of the firm's view of productivity.

The following is a list of behavioral and organizational factors that are possible goals of PG. Organizations can start with this list, but should attempt to add goals of their own.

Strength of Reinforcement. The amount of the bonus can be small or potentially very large. Lincoln Electric has paid bonuses equal to annual pay. Just how much the workforce will be influenced by extrinsic rewards can vary as a function of compensation philosophy, cultural values, and individual differences. It isn't enough to guess that everyone wants a high bonus when some firms have achieved success with small, but well-timed bonuses.

Base of Cooperation. One of the primary advantages of PG plans over individual and group incentive plans is that PG plans provide a common goal among all plan participants. Some PG plans, however, differentially reinforce the idea of cooperation and the base is narrower. Decision makers need to thoroughly discuss how much cooperation will help to meet their productivity goals.

Scope of the Formula. Does the organization want a formula to capture broad areas of productivity or to focus narrowly on, say, cost reduction? The ability of the formula to assist decision makers and any participating employee groups to isolate evolving problems is often overlooked. For example, if quality of product or service is a desired goal because of a well-understood corporate image, a narrow cost reduction PG formula might work against this goal. A more broadly based PG formula that includes market value in its denominator encourages all to share in the final test of the marketplace.

Motivating Harder Work. Is the organization trying primarily to get its workers to work harder? While intuitively it seems organizations always want to encourage employees to work faster, some situations point out this should not be the case. First of all, it may not be possible to get a large increase in speed. In addition, other factors (e.g., safety requirements) may prohibit attempting to achieve this apparently obvious goal. Organizations should seriously evaluate the desire and potential for harder work.

Motivating Smarter Work. Does the organization want to encourage workers to try to come up with better ways to produce goods? While all organizations like to find better ways to produce goods, encouraging workers to develop these items does not come without costs. Obtaining smart ideas from workers includes administration costs. In addition, supervisors may be threatened by workers trying to act smarter. Finally, before organizations try to get workers to act smarter, they should assess the viability of this pursuit. For example, will workers be encouraged to over-control their work?

Motivating Improved Methods. To what degree does the organization believe it can incorporate improved methods? Capital investments and new work arrangements can be a source of increased costs. If management believes that workers can find new ways to improve performance, a series of mechanisms should be included in the PG plan—not the least of which is an appropriate formula.

Motivating Nonlabor Savings. To what degree is it possible for workers to create savings on expenses (e.g., materials, equipment) other than labor? To the extent that such savings are possible, the organization may want to select a formula to reward expense savings that go beyond just labor savings. Organizations should be aware that some complex formulas may come with additional costs—e.g., problems with measurement and communication.

Perceived Fairness of Formula. How important is it to the organization that the formula is fair to different groups of employees? In addition, what is fair? Should all workers receive the same bonus each month or should all employees receive the same percentage of their income? Finally, how important is it that the formula is kept simple so that managers and workers can understand it? In other words, if the formula rewards greater productivity, does it matter that the workers don't understand how the formula works? While organizations would prefer a sound, equitable formula that is simple to understand, the selection of the appropriate PG plan consists of trade-offs. Consequently, it is crucial for the organization to specify the true relative importance of the fairness aspect of potential formulas.

Ease of Administration. While PG plans offer the potential for dramatic increases in productivity, they do require administrative work. Different formulas require different amounts of administrative work. Consequently, organizations need to specify how important it is to minimize administrative complexity. For example, bonuses can be reported and paid weekly or monthly. Information must be collected, processed, and managed. Also, some PG plans involve supervisors heavily in order to explain the formula and related policy.

Economic Flexibility. During the recent recession, a number of PG firms had to cut production dramatically. This, unfortunately, had unexpected impact on the appropriateness of the standards used in the PG formula. If organizations anticipate economic fluctuations to impact the required level of production, a formula should be chosen that (partially) buffers the PG plan from such changes.

Cyclical Variation. Just as economic conditions can effect the appropriateness of the standards used in a PG formula, seasonal variation in organizational production schedules (e.g., number of individuals employed) can also affect the rewards received by workers, independent of their actual efforts. Consequently, an organization needs to consider the amount of seasonal variation in its firm to determine if it wants the formula to address this issue. Obviously, including adjustments for economic and cyclical variation increases the complexity and understandability of the formula.

PROTOTYPIC FORMULAS

The mechanics of PG formula determination typically begin by developing the expected (standard) amount of labor cost necessary to produce a given amount of goods based on historical data. Once the plan is completed, labor actual costs are compared to standard costs for each bonus period (e.g., a week, a month) and the bonus is based on labor cost savings. The five prototypic formulas outlined below vary in terms of what goes into the production costs. Each formula influences the behavioral and organizational factors in different ways. We present sufficient information to allow you the opportunity to understand and evaluate each of them. Before implementation, however, it is appropriate and necessary to examine a more detailed description of the mechanics of the desired formula.

There is no perfect way to measure productivity! Once this statement is accepted, it is possible to rationally examine alternative formulas in order to select the formula with the strongest reinforcement properties for the goals you identified earlier. To evaluate each formula with respect to a given organization, it is important to realize that the advantages and disadvantages of a given formula are only relevant to the extent that they affect the organization. Some of the considerations listed below will not have a serious effect on your organization. Thus, the crucial consideration for an organization is to select the formula with the most advantages and least disadvantages with respect to the target population.

Table 3-1 displays the similar and dissimilar aspects of PG formulas in their prototypic form. For example, the expected amount of labor cost is reflected in the Generalized Base Ratio. This ratio is the input of partic-

TABLE 3-1 Six PG Formulas—A Comparison

		SINGLE RATIO	SPLIT RATIO	MULTICOST RATIO	ALLOWED LABOR	RUCKER/ VALUE ADDED	IMPROSHARE
Generalized Base Ratio	Input	Payroll Costs	Payroll Costs by Product	Labor, Material, Overhead by Product and Department	Actual Labor by Product and Department	Labor	Actual Hours
	Output	Net Sales[a]	Net Sales[a]	Net Sales[a]	Production Standard	Value Added	Total Standard Value Hours

[a]Plus or minus inventories.

Source: B.E. Moore, *Sharing the Gains of Productivity* (Scarsdale, New York: Work in America, 1982).

ular labor costs to the output, as defined by either Net Sales, Production Standard, Value Added, or Total Standard Value Hours. Clearly, each formula shares in common the concept of the base ratio, and thus, a central focus on labor productivity. Each formula varies considerably in the construction of a balance sheet of items that go into making the formula operational. We will review many of these with an eye to the behavioral and organizational factors.

Single Ratio Scanlon Formula

The mechanics of the single ratio formula dictate determining standard labor costs from historical data (preferably over a relatively long time frame) by calculating the percentage of sales that has been used to pay labor expenses (the base ratio). Once this percentage is set, a bonus is earned in any period in which actual labor costs are less than the allowed (standard) rate. For example, assume that historical data prior to the implementation of plan were as shown in Table 3-2.

Now consider a subsequent bonus period (e.g., a month) in which sales value of production is equal to $1,200,000 and labor costs are $210,000. The bonus pool would be equal to:

$$\text{Bonus pool} = \$1,200,000 \times .20 - \$210,000 = \$30,000$$

In actuality, a typical single ratio bonus calculation is straightforward. Table 3-2 illustrates exactly how many companies report their monthly scanlon bonus.

Even this simple (and original) scanlon formula has its policy implications. For example, line 9 reduces the bonus pool by 25%. If this deduction is taken by the firm, it is a hedge against productivity improvements that are not due to labor. Thus, by taking a share of each bonus pool the

TABLE 3-2 Single Ratio Scanlon Formula

1. Sales	$1,100,000
2. Less sales returns, allowances, discounts	25,000
3. Net sales	1,075,000
4. Add: Increase in inventory (at cost or selling price)	125,000
5. Value of production	1,200,000
6. Allowed payroll costs (20% of value of production)	240,000
7. Actual payroll costs	210,000
8. Bonus pool	30,000
9. Company share (25%)	7,500
Subtotal	22,500
10. Reserve for deficit months (25%)	5,625
11. Employee share (75%)—immediate distribution	16,875
12. Participating payroll costs	168,750
13. Bonus percentage ($16,875 ÷ $168,750)	10%

Source: B.E. Moore and T.L. Ross, *The Scanlon Way to Improved Productivity* (New York: Wiley-Interscience, 1978), p. 71.

company is less likely to adjust the base ratio for each technological improvement.

Line 10, Reserve for deficit months, represents a similar hedge for leveling out cyclical variation. In this way, a deduction for periods of very high productivity can be applied to the deficits incurred in periods of very low productivity.

Line 11, Employee share . . . ," reflects $16,875 which is divided by the payroll costs for the period. The result is a 10% bonus applied on top of the actual pay earned during the period. Thus, the bonus is differentially applied in terms of absolute dollars. That is, the plant manager as well as the lowest paid worker receives 10% of monthly salary.

The entire calculation is fairly easy to understand. However, what factors are associated with this formula? Figure 3-1 provides a quick illustration of the optimal levels associated with the single ratio formula. For example, the single ratio formula offers a good measure of performance. Thus, its reinforcement value is good to very good. There is a contingent nature to this calculation that is usually well perceived.

The philosophy of scanlonism stresses cooperation, participation, and involvement to achieve the productivity goals of the firm. The single ratio formula interferes least of all formulas with this message. That is, the simplicity of the formula communicates fairness; i.e., it is not tricky. Connected to this factor is a broad base of cooperation. The formula says,

48

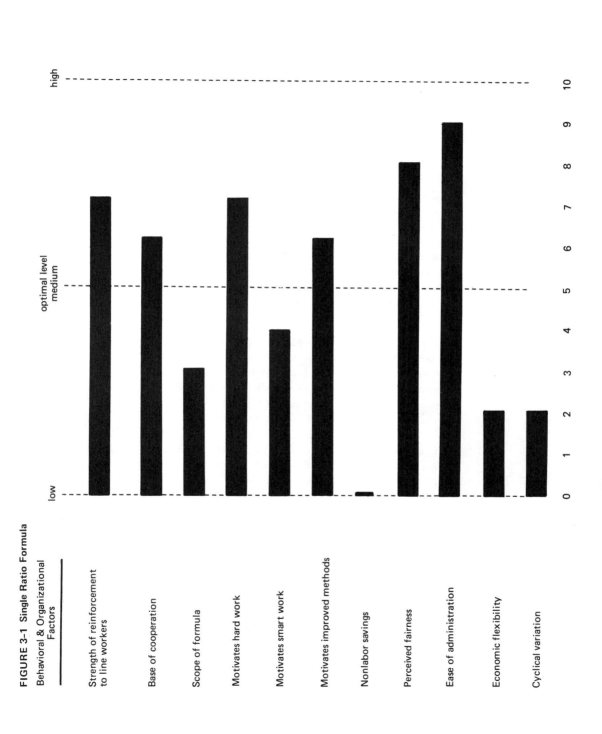

FIGURE 3-1 Single Ratio Formula

"We are all in this together," because virtually all labor and personnel costs are lumped together. Again, the simplicity of the formula makes administration a breeze. However, since the scope of the formula is not as broad as, say, the multicost formula, it does not include a payoff for nonlabor savings. For that reason, the motivation of smarter work is slightly less than average on the optimal level scale. However, the motivation for harder work (i.e., quantity) and for improved methods is more strongly affected by the single ratio formula.

Sudden and significant changes in prices for raw materials can cause the denominator of the simple ratio formula to reflect bonuses incorrectly. It does not have to account for inflation, effects on changes in product mix, technological change, or capital investment. Rapid peaking of cycles of production cannot be easily smoothed by this formula. Thus, both economic flexibility and cyclical variation are handled at a relatively low level of optimality. This is a significant plus when the firm wishes to maximize on trust and understanding.

Split Ratio Formula

Figure 3-2 indicates the optimal levels of behavioral and organizational factors associated with the split ratio formula. This calculation develops the base ratio by product line or other functional cost category. Since this improvement overcomes the single ratio formula problem of changing product mix, it deals more accurately with both economic flexibility and cyclical variation. There is, however, a cost to the ease of administration. And while this formula is inherently fairer, it is more complex. Whereas this formula says, "We are all in this together," it also demonstrates that some product lines contribute more to overall productivity than others. Thus, the base of cooperation may be somewhat affected. This identification of differential product performance may lead to conflict between areas of the firm. While some competition may be beneficial if the conflict is not well managed, lack of cooperation and interdepartmental harassment can result.

In spite of this, we believe the motivational factors as associated with the split ratio formula are about the same as the single ratio formula.

Finally, it is important to understand exactly why the split ratio can be a choice for those firms with sufficient product mix to affect the bonus calculation. Table 3-3 illustrates why the split ratio could be useful. For example, with the single ratio the bonus pool is $60,000. Under the split ratio, the bonus was really $20,000. In this scenario, the single ratio overpaid by $40,000. The true increase to productivity was reflected only in the Product B line.

FIGURE 3-2 Split Ratio Formula

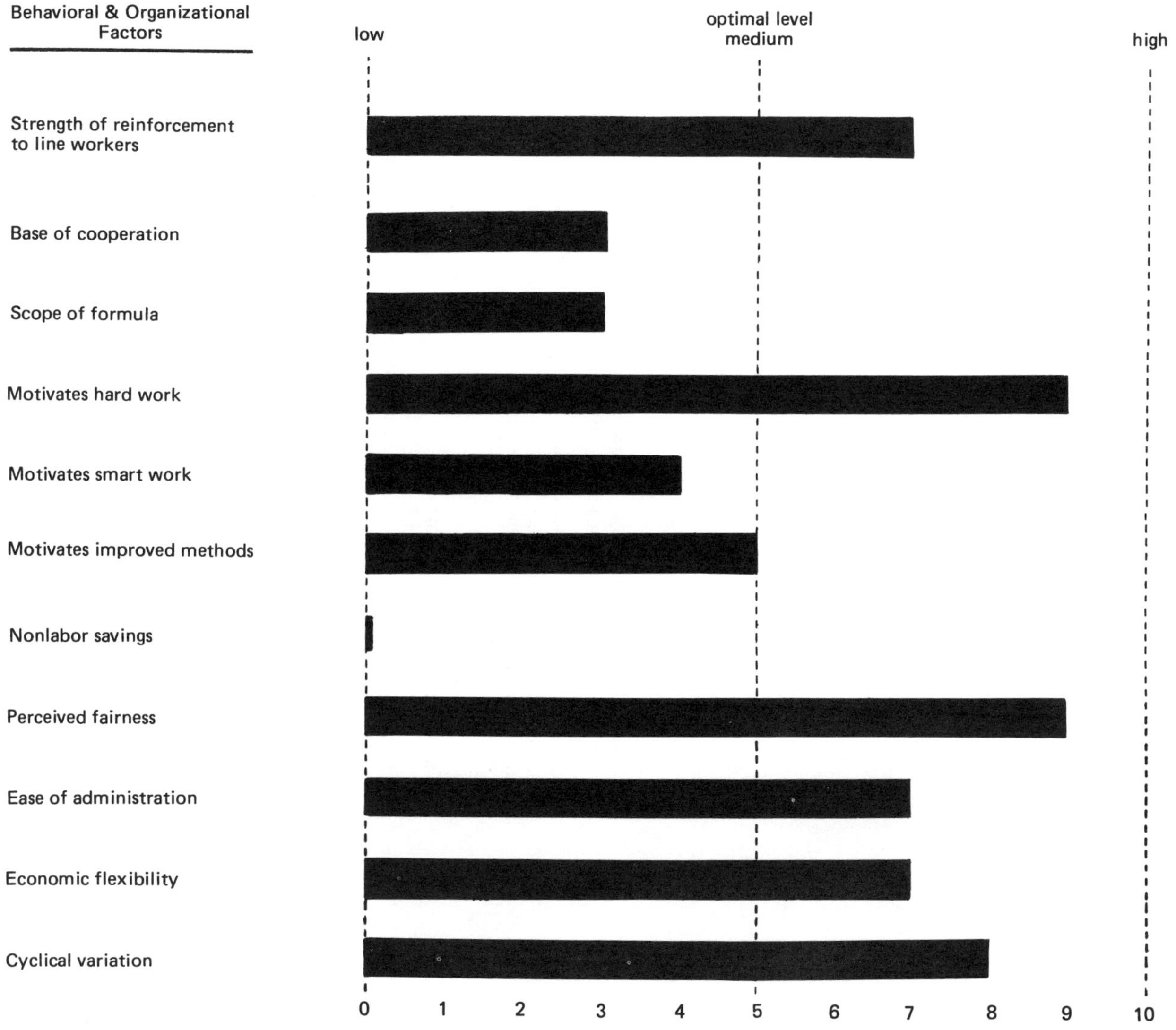

Behavioral & Organizational
Factors

Factor	
Strength of reinforcement to line workers	
Base of cooperation	
Scope of formula	
Motivates hard work	
Motivates smart work	
Motivates improved methods	
Nonlabor savings	
Perceived fairness	
Ease of administration	
Economic flexibility	
Cyclical variation	

low   medium   high
optimal level

0   1   2   3   4   5   6   7   8   9   10

TABLE 3-3 Bonus Calculation Under Single And Assumed Split Ratio Method

PERIOD 1	TYPICAL SINGLE RATIO	SPLIT RATIOS		
		Product A	Product B	Total
Sales value of production	$1,800,000	$1,200,000	$ 600,000	$1,800,000
Allowed payroll costs:				
Single ratio: 20%	360,000			
Split ratio: 10% product A		120,000		
30% product B			180,000	300,000
Actual payroll (assumed)	300,000	140,000	160,000	300,000
Bonus pool	$ 60,000	$ (20,000)	$ 20,000	$ 0

Assumptions:

Period 0
   Two products (A and B) are produced with equal quantities and selling prices.
      Sales of product A = $600,000; sales of product B = $600,000.
   Labor costs allowed = 20% in total; A actually = 10%, B = 30%

Period 1
   Sales of A increase by 100% ($600,000 + $600,000); B's remain the same
      ($600,000).
   Total sales now equal $1,800,000.

Split ratio calculation
   When determining the original allowed amounts, indirect payroll costs were
      allocated to products based on sales and this continues for actual costs in
      subsequent periods.

Source: B.E. Moore and T.L. Ross, *The Scanlon Way to Improved Productivity*
(New York: Wiley-Interscience, 1978), p. 75.

Value-Added (Rucker) Formula

Figure 3-3 illustrates the value-added, or Rucker, formula as it interacts
with the behavioral and organizational factors. The relative strength of its
reinforcement value is equal to the single and split ratio formulas. The base
of cooperation is equal to scanlon-type formulas if involvement systems
accompany this formula.

In fact, most of the behavioral and organizational factors have
similar profiles to those in the single and split ratio formulas. The key
differences are in the area of economic flexibility and cyclical variation.
Most scanlon formulas do not deal well with the inflationary effects on the
sales value of production. Double-digit inflation can undermine the appropriateness of base ratio of most scanlon calculations.

Value-added formulas subtract outside purchases (material and
supplies, energy, etc.) from the sales value of production to determine the
value added by the production process. Based on historical data, allowed
labor costs are computed as a percentage of the value added. This ratio is

52

FIGURE 3-3 Value-Added (Rucker) Formula

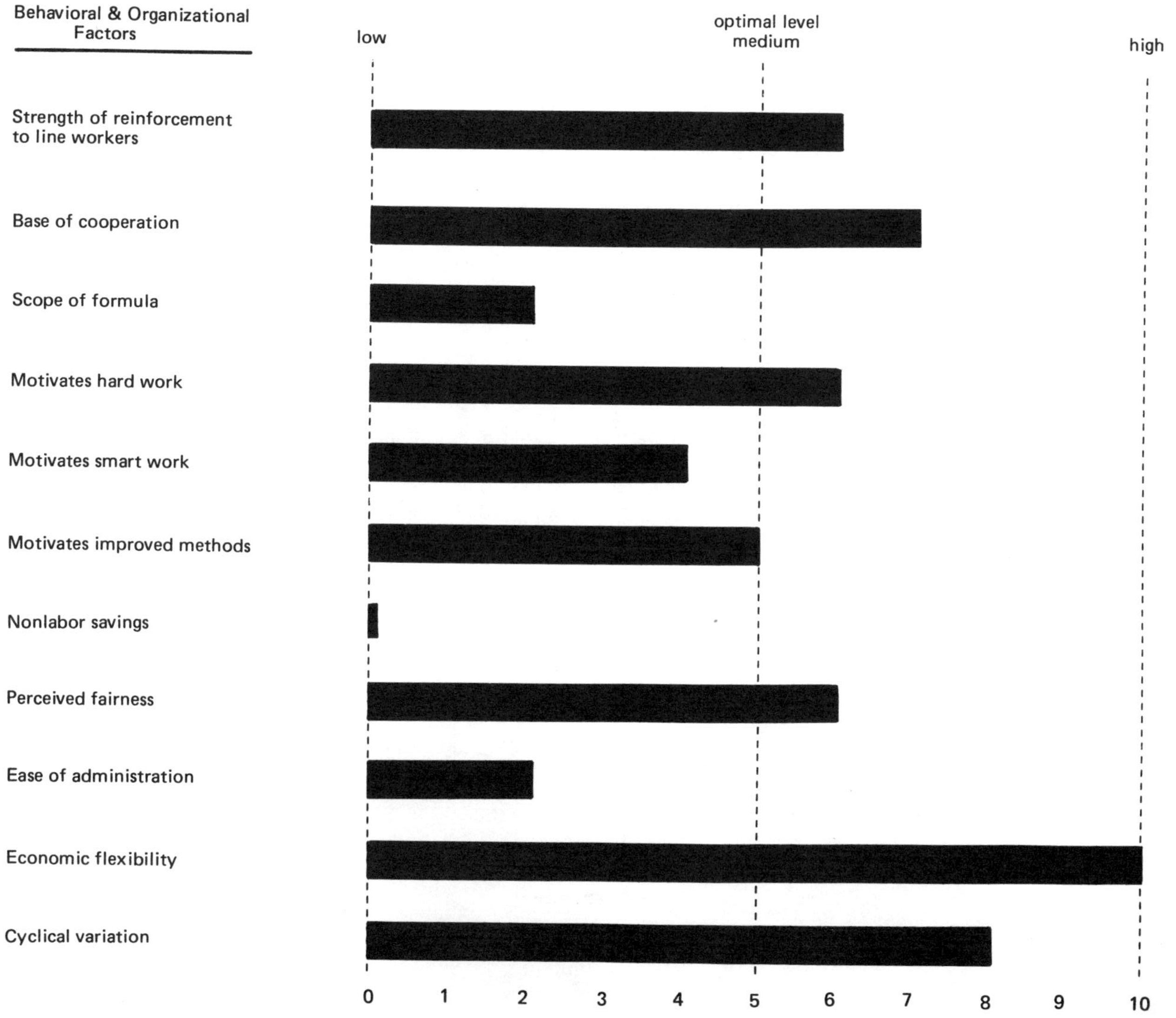

Behavioral & Organizational Factors

Strength of reinforcement to line workers

Base of cooperation

Scope of formula

Motivates hard work

Motivates smart work

Motivates improved methods

Nonlabor savings

Perceived fairness

Ease of administration

Economic flexibility

Cyclical variation

low   optimal level medium   high

0 1 2 3 4 5 6 7 8 9 10

then multiplied by the value added in a particular period and compared to actual labor costs. In comparison to the single ratio formula, the value added formulation deals with product mix and inflation changes by roughly offsetting increased supply costs with increased selling prices. This formula, however, is limited to reinforcing only labor costs analysis, is hard to communicate to employees, and is difficult to administer.

Step 1 of Table 3-4 reflects the difference between the selling price and price adjustments for seasonality. Step 2 reflects subtractions for outside purchases such as materials, supplies, and energy. Value added of $340,000, or 34% of the selling price, is made up of outside purchases. At Step 4 the historical average of labor value added is applied. This is often called the Rucker Standard. In this example, 41.17% ($140,000) is the allowed (or expected) labor cost. Step 5 shows that the actual labor cost was $120,000. Thus, Step 6 reflects a bonus pool of $20,000. A 50/50 split is a common policy and Steps 7 and 8 reflect this. Steps 9 and 10 reflect a policy of a reserve for deficit months (as in the case of many scanlon companies). Since the participating payroll is $80,000 (Step 11), then the bonus percentage becomes 10% in Step 12. The exclusion of outside purchases (Step 12) permits adjustments for inflationary pressures. Also, cyclical variation in other outside purchases and nonlabor costs are kept out of the formula. Thus, Figure 3-3 accurately reflects how these two factors are well handled by the value added formula. For those firms

TABLE 3-4   The Rucker Value-Added Formula

VALUE-ADDED CALCULATION METHOD—MONTH X		
1. Value of production (sales ± various adjustments)		$1,000,000
2. Less Outside purchases (material, supplies, energy)		
Material and supplies	$500,000	
Other outside purchases, nonlabor costs	160,000	660,000
3. Value added (#1 - #2)		340,000
4. Allowed employee costs (from diagnostic historical analysis) #3 X 41.17%)		140,000
5. Actual labor (employee costs)		120,000
6. Bonus pool (#4 - #5)		20,000
7. Company share (50% X #6)		10,000
8. Employee share (#6 - #7)		10,000
9. Reserve for deficit months (20% X #8)		2,000
10. Bonus pool (#8 - #9)		8,000
11. Participating payroll		80,000
12. Bonus percentage (#10 ÷ #11)		10%

Source: B.E. Moore and T.L. Ross, *The Scanlon Way to Improved Productivity* (New York: Wiley-Interscience, 1978) p. 81.

choosing an incentive yet caught by these pressures, this formula requires fewer adjustments.

Multicost Split Ratio Formula

Figure 3-4 depicts the multicost split ratio formula. Notice how the profile of behavioral and organizational factors changes—when compared to the previous formulas. Scope of the formula increases to very high levels since the formula is so comprehensive. Nonlabor savings can now be reinforced since the formula is almost a monthly profit-sharing calculation. Previous formulas cannot reinforce for nonlabor savings. Economic flexibility and the treatment of cyclical variation are handled well. Additionally, the motivation of smarter work gets a boost. Overall, most of the factors increase. However, this is a sophisticated formula requiring excellent accounting and information systems that some firms simply do not have. Also this is not an easy formula to administer—expecially if trust is not high. By way of contrast, the single ratio formula has often been called the simple ratio. Its ease of communication is heightened by its simplicity. When one looks at the multicost split ratio formula, it is readily apparent why its reinforcement value is less. Since reinforcement is one of the primary reasons for choosing a PG plan, this is no small consideration.

Looking more closely at the multicost ratio formula (Table 3-5), we see that it includes all production expenses (labor, materials and supplies, energy, etc.) in the base ratio. This ratio is determined on historical data,

TABLE 3-5 Multicost Ratio Calculation—Month X

1. Value of production (sales ± inventory, allowances, etc.)		$1,000,000
2. Allowable expenses (80% of #1)		800,000
3. Actual expenses:		
Labor (all employee costs)	$120,000	
Material and supplies	500,000	
Other costs (energy, etc.)	160,000	780,000
4. Bonus pool (#2 – #3)		20,000
5. Company share (50% × #4)		10,000
6. Gross bonus		10,000
7. Reserve for deficit months (20% × #6)		2,000
8. Bonus pool (#6 – #7)		8,000
9. Participating payroll		80,000
10. Bonus percentage (#8 ÷ #9)		10%

Source: B.E. Moore and T.L. Ross, *The Scanlon Way to Improved Productivity* (New York: Wiley-Interscience, 1978), p. 79.

FIGURE 3-4 Multicost Split Ratio Formula

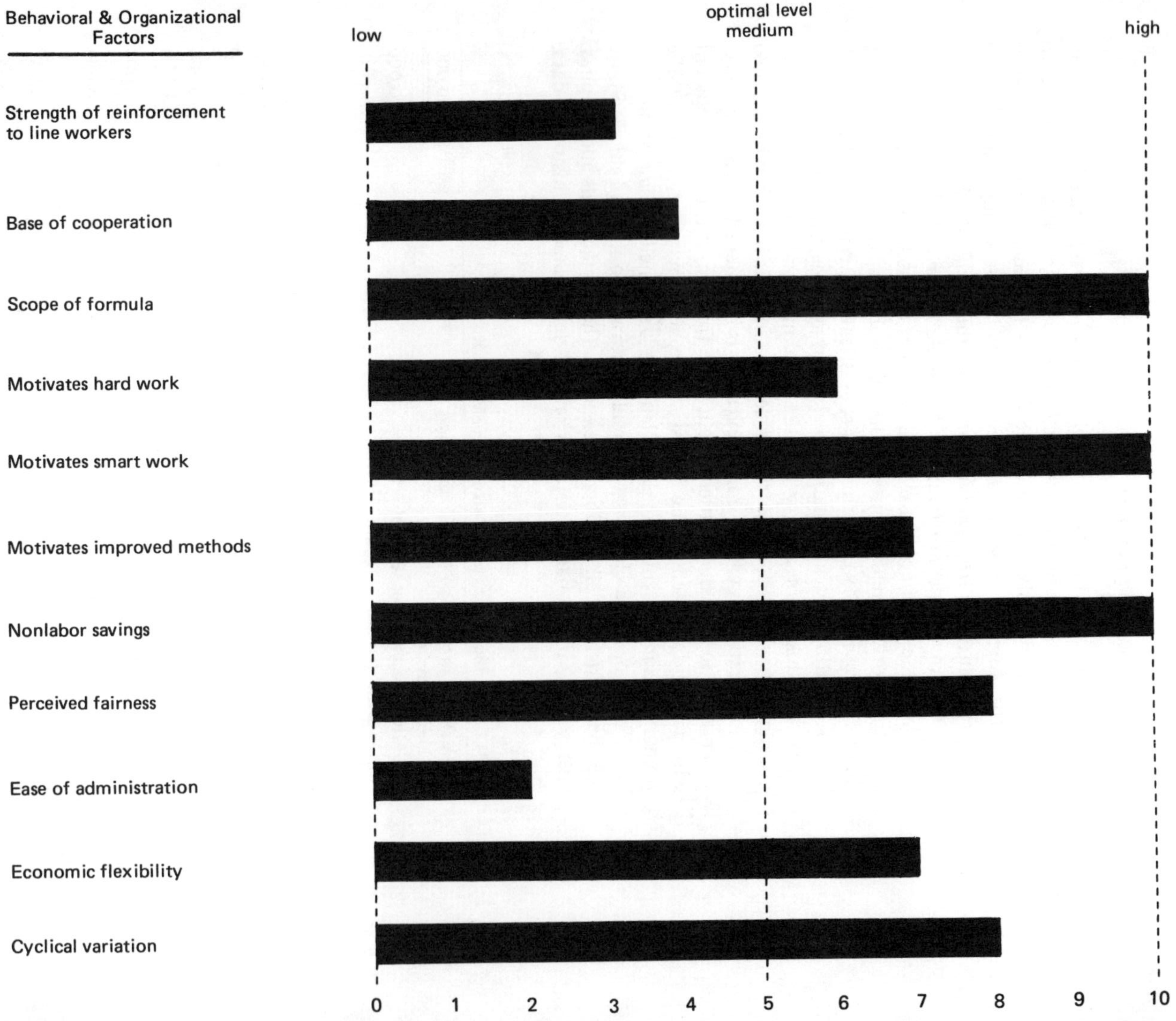

in similar fashion as specified in the single ratio formula section above. The base ratio is determined as follows:

$$\frac{\text{Production expenses (Labor, materials and supplies, energy, etc.)}}{\text{Sales value of production}}$$

During any period in which actual expenses are less than the allowed rate, a bonus is earned. For example, assume that for every $1,000,000 of sales value of production, $800,000 of production expenses were historically incurred. If during a particular period, sales value was equal to $1,100,000, while actual production expenses equaled $780,000 then

$$\text{Bonus pool} = (\$1,000,000 \times .80) - \$780,000 = \$20,000$$

In comparison to the single ratio formula, this formulation offers the advantages of extending the scope of expenses that the workforce is reinforced to reduce. That is, this formulation increases the likelihood of employees finding ways to save nonlabor expenses. The multicost ratio, however, acquires greater administrative costs, is harder to understand, and may frustrate and demotivate workers due to their lack of control over materials, energy, etc.

The multicost formula can also obtain the benefits of the split ratio formula by calculating a sub-bonus pool for each product based on multicosts and adding the sub-bonus pools to obtain the total bonus pool. These advantages, however, obviously incur the problems of the split ratio and multicost formulas.

Moore and Ross strongly recommend that a company new to productivity gainsharing should not start out with a multicost formula.[2] They argue that the formulation is too confusing for employees to relate to and understand. They suggest that organizations desiring a multicost formula should use a two-stage implementation plan, whereby a single ratio is implemented, accepted by the workforce, and then modified to a multicost format.

Improshare

Figure 3–5 displays the behavioral and organizational factors associated with Improshare. This profile is remarkably different from the four previous profiles. For example, it is noticeably easy to administer and has very good reinforcement strength. It is probably true that most firms that pay weekly can and do compute the Improshare on a weekly basis. Most other PG plans cannot compute the bonus that quickly. Since Improshare uses hours worked without regard to sales value of production, this calculation is easily made. Obviously, management must know whether the inventory is selling lest they overproduce and over pay.

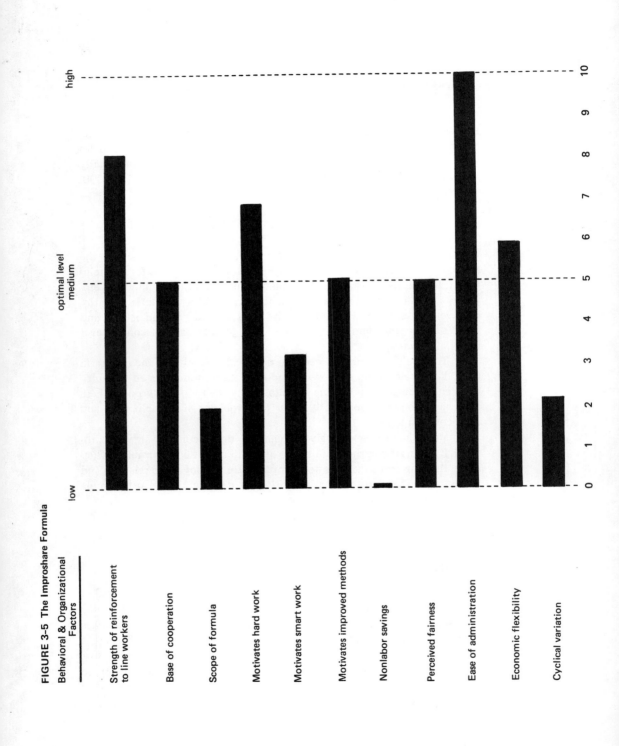

FIGURE 3-5 The Improshare Formula

Behavioral & Organizational Factors

Strength of reinforcement to line workers

Base of cooperation

Scope of formula

Motivates hard work

Motivates smart work

Motivates improved methods

Nonlabor savings

Perceived fairness

Ease of administration

Economic flexibility

Cyclical variation

high

optimal level
medium

low

0 1 2 3 4 5 6 7 8 9 10

Because of its simplicity and usual lack of emphasis on employee involvement, Improshare is relatively easy to install. The plan focuses on the number of work hours saved for a given number of units produced. The actual hours needed to produce a given number of units are subtracted from hours required (or expected) to produce the same number of units. Savings realized by producing a given number of units in reduced hours are shared by the firm and the worker. As mentioned in Chapter 2, there are three key factors to Improshare:

1. Work-hour standards;
2. Base Productivity Factor;
3. Understanding by most workers of the relationship of hours worked to units produced.

By definition, a work-hour standard is the total production hours worked divided by the units produced. The acceptable standard can be produced by engineered standards (e.g., time studies) or by experience data. Either way (or both), it is the norm or expected hours required to produce an acceptable level of output.

Also by definition, the Base Productivity Factor, or BPF, is the total production and nonproduction hours divided by the value of work in work hours (see Table 3-6).

The third key factor associated with Improshare is the simplicity of the formula. Fein has stated that many elements of Improshare's formula have been in use for twenty years.[3] He has assembled a formula that avoids many of the problems of scanlon-type formulas. Since most Americans think in terms of so many hours to produce so many units of work, this formula is psychologically real. There is some evidence to suggest that workers in scanlon firms need to understand the bonus formula.[4,5] In Chapter 2, we argued that the PG formula reinforces the concept of productivity. Many PG firms spend a great deal of time educating the workforce about the formula—often to little avail. Conversely, one study of an Improshare firm shows that line supervisors readily understand and can explain what factors influence the formula.[6]

Fein has pooled all production and nonproduction hours from a selected base period to create the BPF. This is a significant contribution. The BPF, while usually based on time standards, is a composite measure of productive and nonproductive work. Since there are no standards on non-productive work, one necessary assumption is a reasonably constant relationship between productive and nonproductive work. The BPF, therefore, is constructed with data from an average period of productivity, or one that management recognizes as acceptable. Once the BPF is computed it "represents the relationship in the base period between actual hours worked by all employees in the group and the value of the work in man-work hours produced by these employees."[7]

TABLE 3-6   The Improshare Formula

BASE PERIOD OF ACCEPTABLE PRODUCTIVITY

Facts: 40 direct and 20 indirect employees

$$\text{Work hour standard} = \frac{\text{Total production work hours}}{\text{units produced}}$$

$$\text{Product A} = \frac{20 \text{ employees} \times 40 \text{ hours}}{1000 \text{ pieces}} = 0.8 \text{ per piece or } .8 \times 1000 = 800$$

$$\text{Product B} = \frac{20 \text{ employees} \times 40 \text{ hours}}{500 \text{ pieces}} = 1.6 \text{ per piece or } 1.6 \times 500 = 800$$

Total standard value hours 1,600 in Base Period

$$\text{Base Productivity Factor (BPF)} = \frac{\text{Total production and nonproduction hours}}{\text{Total standard value hours}}$$

$$\text{BPF} = \frac{(40 \text{ direct employees} \times 40 \text{ hours}) + (20 \text{ indirect employees} \times 40 \text{ hours})}{\text{actual hours}}$$

$$= \frac{2{,}400 \text{ production hours}}{1{,}600 \text{ standard value hours}} = 1.5$$

BONUS CALCULATION FOR MONTH X

Product A = 0.8 hours × 600 units × 1.5BPF	= 720
Product B = 1.6 hours × 900 units × 1.5BPF	= 2,160
Improshare hours (standard hours for actual units produced)	= 2,880
Less actual hours (assumed)	= 2,280
Gained hours	600

$$\text{Employee share} \left(50\% \text{ of } 600 = \frac{300}{2280} = 13.1\% \right)$$

Source: Adapted from *Productivity Sharing Programs: Can They Contribute to Productivity Improvement?* U.S. General Accounting Office, AFMD-81-22, March 3, 1981: 11.

On balance, Figure 3-5 shows that the profile of optimal levels of behavioral and organizational factors is similar to other PG formulas, but that higher levels are associated with the motivation of hard work (quantity) and ease of administration.

CHOOSING

We have presented five PG formulas with their respective profiles of behavioral and organizational factors. The rational manager should accept the obligation to search for the "best" PG formula based on his or her organizational constraints. As we point out in Chapter 1, this process requires a thorough understanding of where the firm is, who its people are, and how it expects to achieve its objectives.

In summary, formula selection is a crucial step in developing a PG plan. The formula should optimally reinforce the goals of the firm, rather than result from the simple minded acceptance of the suggestion of the favorite formula of a "known" consultant. In this chapter, we have identified a number of goals that an organization should consider in identifying their goal profile. In addition, we have examined the performance of a number of prototypic formulas in achieving these goals. The most difficult step remains: The firm must evaluate and honestly determine their goal profile and the relative importance of alternate goals. The firm will then be in a position to use our diagnostic aid to optimally select a formula for their PG plan.

NOTES

1. Brian E. Moore, and Timothy L. Ross, *The Scanlon Way to Improved Productivity* (New York: Wiley-Interscience, 1978).

2. Ibid.

3. Mitchell Fein, "An Alternative to Traditional Managing," in *Handbook of Industrial Engineering*, ed. Gavriel Salvendy (New York: Wiley, 1981).

4. Frederick G. Lesieur, ed., *The Scanlon Plan: A Frontier in Labor-Management Cooperation* (Cambridge: Technology Press of M.I.T. and New York: John Wiley & Sons, 1958).

5. Timothy L. Ross, and G.M. Jones, "An Approach to Increased Productivity: The Scanlon Plan," *Financial Executive*, February 1972, pp. 23–29.

6. Ruben S. Alanis and Brian E. Moore, "Organizational Learning of New Incentive System: Improshare" (Manuscript, The University of Texas at Austin, 1981).

7. Fein, "An Alternative," p. 343.

4

Ten Years of Experience with the Scanlon Plan: DeSoto Revisited

by Brian E. Graham-Moore

In 1970, after presenting a lecture on incentives to an evening class of M.B.A. students at the University of Chicago, a student asked me if I was interested in scanlon plans. That student proved to be Richard Anderson, general manager of Chemical Coatings Division, DeSoto, Inc. On his invitation I was present when Fred Lesieur explained how the scanlon plan would increase productivity for DeSoto. At the end of the meeting, I was asked for my opinion. Not only was I convinced that this form of PG was potentially useful, but I also offered to evaluate how and why the plan was to be learned so that other DeSoto manufacturing units could benefit from the first installation. That same day, I met Tom Lester, then general manager of DeSoto Co., Southwest. Tom had wanted a scanlon plan even before corporate management. It was soon decided that DeSoto Southwest, in Garland, Texas, would be the first experimental site and that Dr. Paul S. Goodman (now at Carnegie-Mellon University) and I would have a free hand to design a complete evaluation study to focus on what is learned, who learns, and whether learning the principles of PG influences productivity.

DeSoto, unlike some firms that are drawn to PG, is a quality corporation. That is, DeSoto management is top caliber. DeSoto has always had a commitment to full employment. Its compensation and fringe benefits lead the paint industry. Virtually all of DeSoto's product is sold as private label to Sears. Yet, DeSoto strives for continued excellence. It was not surprising that management was drawn to the scanlon plan.

The original study indicated remarkable changes in attitudes and increased productivity during the trial year of 1971.[1] In 1972, I left Chicago for the University of Texas at Austin. At Tom Lester's invitation I continued to monitor the Garland site. During the years of 1972-74, I also studied DeSoto plants at Chicago Heights, Illinois; Greensboro, North Carolina; and Columbus, Ohio. All have patterned successful scanlon plans after the Garland plant. In the ensuing years, I have visited and communicated frequently with the management and workforce at the Garland plant. This case study recounts one of the few longitudinal studies of a scanlon plan. It is only possible due to the cooperation and kind assistance of the personnel of DeSoto, Inc., Garland, Texas. To them, I extend my most grateful thanks.

KEY ASPECTS OF DeSOTO'S PLAN

Before proceeding with DeSoto's experience with the scanlon plan, a clear description of their plan is necessary. DeSoto's scanlon plan is a company-wide productivity improvement plan. It consists of three basic elements: A philosophy of cooperation, an involvement system designed to increase efficiency and reduce costs, and a formula that permits a bonus to be paid based on increases in productivity.

DeSoto's Philosophy. Employer-employee cooperation is essential. Teamwork is promoted in the belief that both worker and manager have valuable information to share. This sharing of knowledge provides the worker with the means to collaborate and cooperate with management. Management leads, but the workers actively participate.

DeSoto's Involvement System. A new committee structure was established in the organization and thus became a new mechanism for communication. This structure facilitates the communication, evaluation, and disposition of suggestions. Two kinds of committees were organized. A production committee was formed in each department or working unit and consisted of carefully selected workers. The screening committee consisted of management and selected members from the production committees. The functions and authority of both committees is covered in greater detail in Moore and Ross.[2]

DeSoto's Formula. A baseline measurement of productivity was necessary in order to pay bonuses for any increase in productivity. Normal labor costs were determined before installing the plan so that a ratio of labor costs to sales value of products manufactured could be formulated. The base ratio was determined between (1) total labor costs, including factory and salary payroll, vacations, and holidays, and (2) sales value of production, including adjustments for such items as inventory fluctuations price variations. The formula relates total personnel costs to the sales value of production.

$$\text{Base ratio} = \frac{\text{Total personnel costs of items to be included}}{\text{Sales + inventory changes}}$$
(finished and work-in-process inventories)

This relationship between the human resource cost and the production value is the normal ratio of labor to output, or the base ratio. Any increase in the denominator (sales value of production) relative to the numerator (total personnel costs) represents an increase in productivity. This increase is a bonus to be distributed to everyone on the participating payroll. Therefore, with the entire organization focusing its attention on this relationship between human resource investment and productivity, the formula encouraged employees to learn more productive behaviors, in order to do better than the base ratio.

These three elements (the philosophy of cooperation, the involvement system, and the formula) make up what is generally known as the scanlon plan. DeSoto's experience with the plan is an example of a well-managed firm that is successful in increasing its productivity goals.

PRODUCTIVITY OUTCOMES AT DeSOTO

Figure 4-1 represents the average bonus percent of annual pay from 1971 to 1981 at DeSoto. The range of average bonus for this eleven-year period is from 2 + % to 21 + % (the average for all years is 7.8%). This bonus is usually paid as a percentage of pay earned in a given month by each employee, i.e., managers, technicians, and hourly employees. Monthly bonuses at DeSoto ranged from 0% to 21.78%. That means that during a highly productive period, DeSoto was able to provide a bonus of 21.78% to everyone based on each person's monthly pay plus overtime. Monetary benefits are not the only rewards provided by the plan. There are numerous intangible benefits resulting from the plan which will be covered in a later section of this report.

A cost-accounting analysis of the plan is reflected in Table 4-1. The figures are disguised since the absolute values are privileged information. However, the percent increase in payroll and percent increase in productivity are accurate. Thus, one can readily see that the increases in produc-

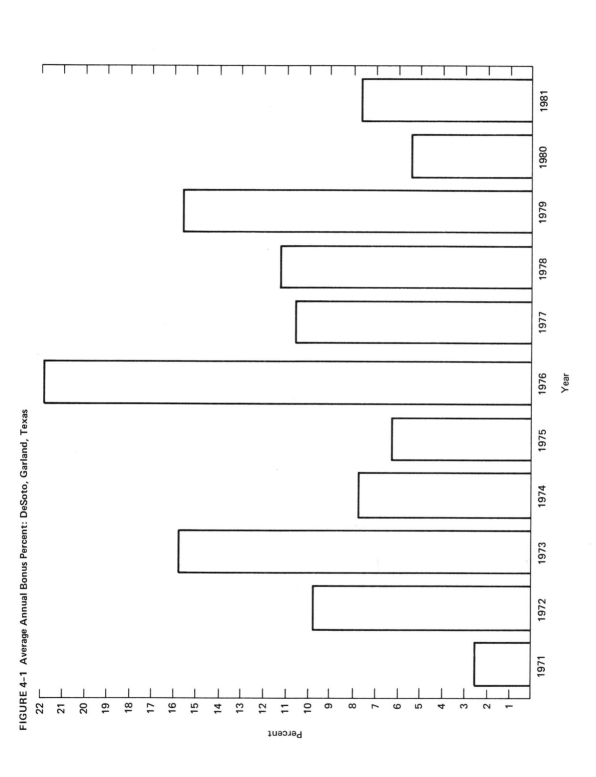

FIGURE 4-1 Average Annual Bonus Percent: DeSoto, Garland, Texas

TABLE 4-1 Scanlon Plan—Annual Comparison to Base Year

LINE	1980	1979	1978	1977
1. Scanlon Payroll w/ Bonus	$ 7,957,247	$ 8,503,296	$ 7,827,629	$ 7,118,861
2. Scanlon Payroll w/o Bonus	7,562,306	7,455,641	7,075,141	6,522,186
3. Gallons Produced	26,562,306	33,298,073	29,708,114	30,545,550
4. Cost per Gallon w/ Bonus	74.6	62.8	64.8	57.3
5. Cost per Gallon w/o Bonus	70.9	55.1	58.6	52.7
6. Percent Increase in Payroll	1%	5%	9%	8%
7. Hours Worked	1,001,556	1,006,825	1,033,243	1,012,364
8. Gallons per Hour	64.4	81.5	85.6	74.3
9. Percent Increase in Productivity	41%	78%	45%	52%

tivity are substantial when compared to the necessary increase in payroll costs.

Table 4-1 presents figures for 1970, the last year of operation before the plan. The "actual" payroll with and without the bonus is shown on lines 1 and 2. The output measure of gallons produced in 1970 (line 3) was approximately 18.4 million. Except for 1971, it has continued to increase at a fairly steady rate. No major changes in technology accompanied this increase, so it may be concluded that the plan has been a significant factor in causing this increase in productivity. Lines 6 and 9 are of critical interest in that they represent the ratio of the necessary increase in payroll costs and the resulting increase in productivity. The most recent figures (1980) reflect a 1% increase in payroll in 1970 dollars and a 41% increase in productivity.

Care must be exercised in the interpretation of any measure of productivity since output per man-hour can be influenced by many factors. Obviously the plan is one of these factors. At this point in time, it is difficult to determine just how great a role the plan plays at DeSoto in increasing productivity. However, the intangible benefits provided solely by the plan are more than enough to justify its existence and provide a reason for its continuation at DeSoto.

Large and rapid changes in prices for raw materials is a special issue associated with the productivity formula. When these changes occur, the equity of the original formula is disturbed. Management must then adjust the ratio in order to keep it closely tied to true productivity. However, if the formula is constantly being changed, employee trust will diminish. So, as has been the policy at DeSoto, management should exercise great caution and forethought before instigating any change in the productivity formula.

Another kind of problem DeSoto was forced to deal with was the mix in labor costs. As in many manufacturing concerns, some products are buyouts; that is much or all of a product is produced elsewhere and is only

1976	1975	1974	1973	1972	1971	1970
$ 6,247,231	$ 4,985,356	$ 4,743,234	$ 4,652,885	$ 4,332,199	$ 3,793,478	$ 3,945,603
5,186,415	4,705,865	4,422,616	4,063,433	3,969,010	3,708,700	3,945,603
25,851,557	21,530,799	20,765,487	22,480,450	20,659,223	16,439,123	18,447,046
59.6	56.8	56.1	50.9	51.7	55.6	52.7
49.5	53.9	52.4	44.5	47.3	56.8	52.7
17%	5%	6%	12%	8%	2%	
858,781	856,595	878,606	852,414	863,796	871,511	992,524
74.1	61.8	58.1	65.0	58.8	46.8	45.8
40%	17%	13%	22%	12%	11%	

handled by DeSoto. Thus, the labor content in buyouts is lower than produced products. In order for the productivity formula to be fair, this issue should be considered and reflected in the formula. Specific formula changes that have occurred at DeSoto and trust in the fairness of management have been maintained. Clearly, if the objective of the formula is to reward cooperative efforts and true productivity, then equity for both management and workers is important. The worker must trust management's construction and calculation of the formula. On the other hand, management must not feel that the formula is a giveaway. Indeed, one of the concerns of DeSoto management about the plan has been the efficacy of the formula. This proves to be an empirical problem, answerable only when the accounting data are assembled.

To summarize, the purpose of the formula and its accurate formulation is equity—a fair share for all. As it has been stated:

> If the employees decide favorably and the formula is arrived at from the historical accounting facts, then the ratio is set at the most representative position consistent with current market and production demands. The ratio position is the best judgment for the equity of all employees. The ratio is subject to continuous study and evaluation to insure the optimal equity of everyone. If the ratio jeopardized the company's fiscal and competitive position, the deficiency in equity for all is recognized and the ratio is appropriately modified. If the ratio severely disadvantages the employee investors, the inequality is clearly defined and the appropriate change is made.[3]

INVOLVEMENT SYSTEM AS STRUCTURE AND PROCESS

Often overlooked and sometimes overstated, the involvement system is the structure and process of the plan. There are few in-depth studies of this system. Therefore, understanding the characteristics of the system, as exemplified at the DeSoto plant, is the objective of this section.

At the DeSoto plant the plan was introduced by Fred Lesieur, a highly skilled consultant in the specific field of scanlon plans. The introductory process at DeSoto included the three steps basic to any scanlon plan introduction:

1. presentation of the three components of the plan, i.e., the philosophy, the involvement system, and the formula;
2. election (companywide) to determine if the plan will be instituted for a trial year;
3. installation of the productivity formula and the involvement system, assuming a positive vote.

These steps appear simple. But it is important to remember that each one of them is itself a detailed process requiring careful execution. DeSoto management spent a great deal of time discussing exactly how these steps would be achieved.

After the introduction process was completed, the next step was to staff the production and screening committees. A description of the production and screening committees, their governing procedures, and guidelines for handling suggestions was distributed to the workforce in order to help them understand the plan. Management then decided on the number of production committees needed (eight—one for each department) and the number of committee members needed to ensure balanced representation among departments, shifts, and job levels (three to five committee members per department depending on the size of the department and the number of night shift workers). A provision was made for the numbers to be changed at a later time if the circumstances warranted.

DeSoto management felt that representation was essential to the success of the plan for two reasons. First, it guaranteed good representation of ideas. By making certain all functional units of the company were represented, the involvement system was ensured of obtaining input that could reflect the differing viewpoints of all employees. Second, good representation aids in the process of peer review. Critical evaluation of all suggestions on many different levels is made possible through adequate representation of the workforce.

A production committee was established within each department or functional area of the company. The purpose of the committee is to use workers' ideas about how to improve the performance of their jobs. The production committee consists of the departmental supervisor and at least one employee representative. Suggestions for improved operations are presented to the production committee. At least once a month the production committee reviews the suggestions that have been submitted. Suggestions not affecting other departments and not exceeding a specified dollar amount ($200) are put into effect at the departmental level by the production committee. Also, any suggestion rejected at the production committee level always receives another hearing by the screening committee.

The screening committee is made up of 50% management and 50% representatives from the production committees. Its three main activities are to (1) review and evaluate suggestions, (2) announce the bonus (or deficit), and (3) discuss the reasons for the bonus (or deficit).

The purpose of reviewing and evaluating suggestions is to process all relevant information and to guarantee that collective points of view intersect at the point of decision. The final decision, however, is the plant manager's.

Tom Lester, DeSoto's plant manager, felt that immediate feedback is necessary in order for the plan to be effective. The announcement of the bonus (or deficit) provides this feedback. Each department or functional area has one representative who listens to controller Jim Barker's scanlon report. Then the representatives leave the meeting and announce the bonus (or deficit) in their respective work areas.

The third principal activity of the screening committee, discussing the reasons for the bonus (or deficit), includes a discussion of how the bonus (or deficit) affects the company and its objectives in terms of production, costs, and so on. This activity is exemplified by the following portion taken from a DeSoto screening committee meeting.

> *Tom Lester:* Our orders normally fall off in June when we add summer workers to cover vacations. Naturally, personnel costs will go up while sales are expected to decline below our normal base ratio. Folks ought to know we expect deficits no matter how much harder and smarter they work.

> *Production Committee*
> *Member:* Maybe we could get by with fewer summer workers since our productivity is higher?

> *Personnel Manager:* It's worth a try, Tom. We might get by with one half the number we normally hire—if everyone understands that this will reduce expected deficits.

> *Tom Lester:* Well, could we talk this up on the floor to see how people feel?

Within a mature scanlon company, the discussion of why a firm can or cannot achieve its goals surfaces within the screening committee meetings. As a result of these discussions, the screening committee becomes a task-oriented classroom for combining individual and corporate goals to achieve success. With a consultant's help, DeSoto developed specific procedures offered for handling suggestions. Explanation of these procedures should provide the reader with a global overview of the involvement system, and more importantly, how the production and screening committees make this system work.

Although concrete procedures for handling suggestions are described, it is the process of handling them that insures the involvement system. In other words, one should always keep in mind that these procedures are by no means absolute. The important thing is that DeSoto managers make every effort to deal with people face to face in all aspects of the suggestion-making process. By doing this, lines of communication are developed and expanded on at all job levels. The involvement system provides an employee not only with the opportunity to exchange ideas with his peers but, more importantly, to exchange ideas with his supervisors. In this respect the scanlon plan offers the distinct advantage of increased communication that leads to increased employee participation in the overall attainment of company objectives. The procedures that follow should not become a bureaucratic device that interferes with or takes the place of open communication.

1. Someone with a suggestion should submit it in writing to a departmental representative.
2. The supervisor or departmental representative should discuss the suggestion with the person making it, and others who may be affected, and take appropriate action as soon as possible.
3. Meeting at least once a month, both committees should review the status of previously discussed suggestions, should expedite delayed suggestions, and should discuss new suggestions.
4. Suggestions involving more than the specified dollar amount (more than $200 at DeSoto) should be referred to the screening committee.
5. The production committee should assign the responsibility for following through on delayed suggestions to one of its members.
6. The production committee should keep records of its activities. These records should include all submitted suggestions and their status—action proposed, action taken, and so on.
7. By a certain day of the month, the production committee should submit all suggestions received during that month to the screening committee.
8. All suggestions and actions taken by the production committee should be reported to the screening committee monthly.

The production committee can take one of five actions on the suggestions it receives:

1. Reject suggestion with carefully stated reasons.

2. Accept suggestion and use it.

3. Accept suggestion and place it under investigation. (A suggestion is normally placed under investigation when there is insufficient information to make a decision or when it is necessary to ascertain if net savings offset the cost of implementing the suggestion).

4. Accept suggestion by recommending it to the screening committee. (Such a suggestion is usually that which a production committee feels should be placed into effect but costs over the specified dollar amount).

5. If production committee members cannot agree on the acceptability of a suggestion, it is referred to screening committee.

In summary, the involvement system is a new committee structure superimposed on the organization to facilitate communication, evaluation, and disposition of suggestions. As mentioned, two kinds of committees are established—production and screening. Obviously, the involvement system is an integral part of the scanlon plan. The production committee and screening committee coupled with employee participation and cooperation help determine the success of the plan. For this reason, it is important that all employees have a basic understanding of this system and how it operates.

Personnel Manager Bob Highland developed these guidelines for production committee members. As they are elected to their positions, they meet with Highland to review and discuss these responsibilities:

> As the Production Committee Representative you will have certain responsibilities in coordinating the Scanlon activities for your department. Since you were elected as the representative for your department by your fellow employees, it will be necessary for you to spend some time in soliciting suggestions, following through on suggestions, giving clear and accurate reports to your group as to the status of their suggestions, and also doing your homework for the Screening Meeting. Remember your fellow employees are counting on you!

1. *How much money can we spend to implement a suggestion?* Production Committees are authorized to spend up to $200; Department Heads up to $400; and the Plant Manager is authorized on expenditures up to $500. Any expenditure of more than $500 would require capital expenditure and need to be budgeted.

2. *When should our Production Committee Meeting be held?* This meeting can be held any time prior to the Screening Committee Meetings. It probably would be helpful if you held the meeting two or three days before the Screening Meeting so you can do some last-minute checking. You may also wish to hold more than one meeting in a month, if suggestion activity warrants it.

3. *Where should our meeting be held?* The meeting can be held anywhere at any time. The most important thing is that we meet!

4. *How soon should a suggestion be put "in use"?* If a suggestion is made and has merit, don't wait for a Production Meeting or a Screening Meeting to implement. If the cost is within your expenditure guidelines, get it working.

5. *What should be covered at our meeting?* It is most important to review the status of all active suggestions. Be prepared for the Screening Meeting with quotes, maintenance schedules, and the present status of the suggestion. The key is to act and keep the suggestion moving.

6. *If a suggestion needs to be investigated, what should we do?* On suggestions requiring an investigation, assign an investigation team, and list these employees so their names are typed on the minutes. It is very important that all investigation team members be notified and asked to investigate a suggestion and gather all the pertinent facts concerning the suggestion. If members of other departments are concerned, be sure to notify the appropriate people.

7. *What should I report at the Screening Meeting?* At the Screening Committee Meeting, it is not necessary to read the entire suggestion, but only to refer to the suggestion number and report on the disposition. It is most important to give as much information about a suggestion as possible. If you need to refer a suggestion for additional approval for expenditures, do so at this meeting. Remember your committee can spend $200, and department heads may approve $400 in expenditures.

8. *What should I report to my department after a Screening Committee meeting?* At the Employee Information meeting give the bonus disposition and the status of the reserve account. Also review the status of all suggestions, and be sure the individual who made the suggestion has an explanation of the disposition. This includes giving the reason for a rejection in the event the suggestion is not approved, or the status of the suggestion at the present time. This is most important since there is not a suggestion as important as our own.

RESULTS OF SUGGESTION-MAKING PROCESS

The process of group suggestion making at DeSoto involves the entire organization in new ways regardless of the prevailing organizational climate or managerial style. As a result of this process, the rates of all organizational interactions increase worker to worker, worker to supervisor, and worker to management. Increased interaction is only one of the many outcomes which are the result of this structure and process, but it is revealing to do an in-depth analysis of one of the results of this process—the suggestions themselves. Suggestions are classified by their content. The content analyses allow numerous inferences to be made and provide even greater insight into the plan and its overall effect on the organization. A management committee (consisting of the plant manager, the controller, and the personnel manager) was established at the DeSoto plant for the purpose of evaluating suggestions. Also, the participation of the technical director of the plant was especially helpful. The results of these analyses are depicted in Figures 4-2 and 4-3.

Figure 4-2 indicates that all suggestions of the trial year (1971) fall into one of four categories. Multiple-category suggestions were tallied in their primary category. The first category is irritants, i.e., suggestions that improve working conditions, but not necessarily the quality or quantity of the product being manufactured. Categories represented in Figure 4-2 are (1) quantity, suggestions that increase the number of units manufactured; (2) quality, suggestions that increase the product value so that it will obtain a higher price or draw fewer complaints; and (3) cost reduction, suggestions that increase the use of waste-reducing methods, the conservation of raw materials, and the conservative use of resources allocated for overhead costs. McKersie states that most workers focus on cost reduction suggestions.[4] (4) The last category reflects suggestions that are not productivity related, i.e., irritants.

During the first three months of 1971 there were 91 suggestions, which involved the majority of the workforce. By the end of the trial year, 82% of the workforce at DeSoto had made at least one suggestion. These facts clearly indicate that the installation of this type of system does increase communication within an organization. The involvement and participation of all employees within the organization is a result of refining, processing, deciding, and feeding back the disposition of all suggestions. In other words, the involvement and participation of all employees is a result of open communication.

Also, Figure 4-2 indicates that in the first three months of operation under the plan, irritations with the working conditions at DeSoto dominated the suggestions made by the employees. This situation is to be expected for two reasons: (1) suggestion making is a new activity, and common sources of ideas come from the irritants (the dissatisfiers that exist in the work environment); and (2) time is required for the consultant, management, and the committee system to determine which suggestions influence the bonus. Because production committees can implement some suggestions immediately, they are required to look at costs. It is at this time that employees, at all levels, become aware of the true effect of a given suggestion and priorities are established. This learning process helps reduce the flow of suggestions, since only productivity-improvement suggestions are sought.

As suggestions are taken care of and as suggestions for quantity, quality, and cost are processed, ideas seem to dry up. A factor that seems

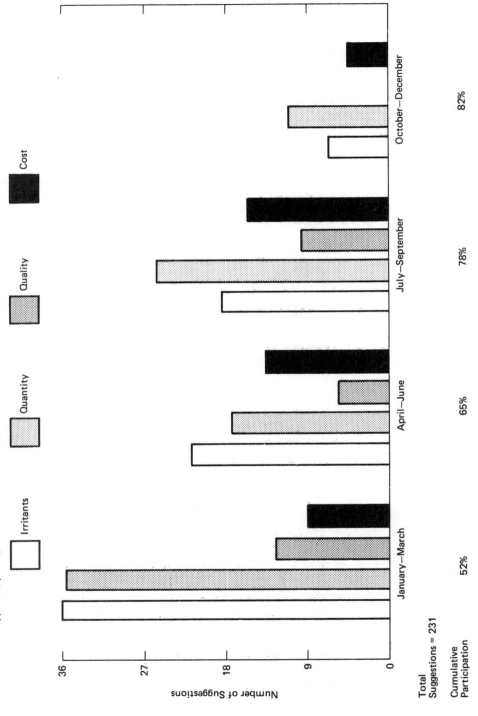

FIGURE 4-2 Type of Suggestion and Degree of Participation Over Time. [Source: B. E. Moore, "A Plant-Wide Productivity Plan in Action: Three Years of Experience with the Scanlon Plan" (Washington, D.C., The National Commission on Productivity and Work Quality, 1975) p. 14.]

to influence the rate of suggestion making is the ability of the organization to institute good suggestions. For example, when business conditions are not expanding, management is reluctant to make a capital investment on worthy suggestions. Also economies of scale necessary to make suggestions profitable must exist. Holding up a suggestion implies to the suggester that future attempts at suggestion making have a reduced probability of being accepted. Thus, the involvement system becomes a source of learning about the factors in the organization that affect productivity.

FIGURE 4–3 Type of Suggestion by Number of Suggestions Yearly: DeSoto, Garland, Texas

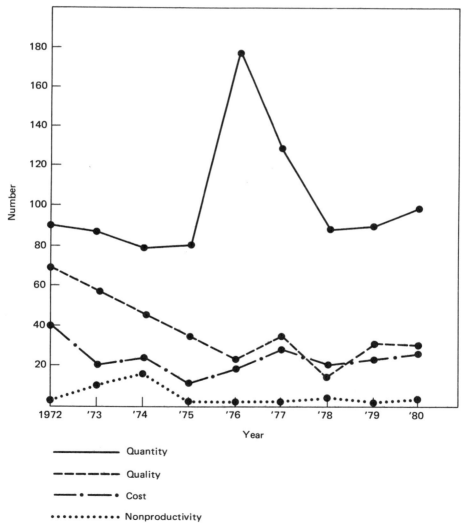

Figure 4–3 provides an extended look at suggestion-making activity over a nine-year period at DeSoto. The Irritants category in Figure 4–2 is changed to nonproductivity-related (NP) suggestions. The only reason for this change is that careful analysis of the suggestions indicates that most NP suggestions are related to safety rather than irritations with the work environment. All NP suggestions are accepted into the system as this is the philosophy of the plan. However, NP suggestions are referred to safety committees. Also, NP suggestions that could be classified as grievances are dealt with outside of the involvement system. Thus, grievance procedures are not handled under the plan.

The main story in Figure 4–3 is that quantity suggestions lead in all years (1972–79), continuing the trend from the trial year (1971). The percentage of participation of productivity-related suggestions (quantity, quality, and cost) ranges from 53% to 91% over the eight-year time span. At certain times during this period, NP suggestions outnumber quality or cost suggestions, but never the total number of productivity-related suggestions. There are several reasons for this occurrence. First, careful review of the literature has shown that periods of favorable economic activity, good markets, and other external environmental factors co-vary with the type of suggestions made. That is to say that increased productivity focuses worker attention on how to increase quantity, improve quality, and reduce costs. During slack periods there may be high rates of suggestion making, but productivity-related suggestions are more difficult to make and implement. Examples of the different types of suggestions made at different economic time periods are provided below.

Slack Period: "Have a bonus of $3.00 or $4.00 a week if you are not late or absent from work."

Disposition: Rejected. It is the employee's responsibility to work every day and arrive on time.

Busy Period: "Tanks D-61, 62, and 70; install 2″ valve on bottom of tanks for draining off materials. Understand this was approved first year of Scanlon, but never completed."

Disposition: Accepted. S. will see that this is done over a period of time.

Slack-period suggestions in mature plan organizations such as DeSoto signify search behavior on the part of well-motivated employees. However, DeSoto management believe it is often unrealistic to expect useful suggestions during this time. Problem-solving behavior requires problems that are immediate and implementable. Conversely, the busy-period suggestion making exemplifies the immediacy of this type of problem solving. In slack periods, it does not matter as much how quickly the tanks are turned around. However, when production picks up, the productivity-minded worker sees that a larger valve would increase quantity by speeding up drain time. Obviously, a relationship exists between outside forces of demand and inside problem-solving focused on problems of immediacy.

Major developments within the organization are a second reason for significant changes in the suggestion mix. These developments include such things as an addition of a new department or work area, technological changes in production, and turnover in management or supervisory-level positions. Figure 4-3 represents this situation very clearly. Looking at the 1976 data, a significant increase in quantity suggestions occurred. This can be attributed to the addition of a new latex department within the DeSoto plant.

When talking about the structure of the involvement system, the amount of time spent on committee meetings is a constant source of discussion. The screening committee at DeSoto spends one to two hours per month on prescribed duties. Production committees meet officially at least once a month for 10 minutes to one hour. Meetings are scheduled at slow periods, yet, breaks, lunch periods, and even car pools also provide opportunities for the discussion of suggestions. Also, many suggestions are made by groups, representing the culmination of much "pilot-testing" behavior.

DeSoto management raised the question, How do group suggestion systems compare with individual suggestion systems? It discovered that group suggestion systems, such as the plan, are difficult to cost out. There is no cost measurement employed in this system. On the other hand, there is the formula of 10% of the estimated cost savings of a suggestion applied to most individual suggestion systems. Using this formula, firms can actually generate a dollar amount of estimated savings. Proponents of the plan would expect a greater saving, arguing that individual suggestion systems encourage withholding information.

A multivariate analysis of 200 U.S. firms with individual suggestion systems revealed the following. Regardless of the type of industry, type of suggestion system administration, or some 70 other variables, the principal finding was that a strong norm appeared to govern the payout for suggestions.[4] This lack of variability of suggestion award payouts combined with the low acceptance less than 30% of eligibles who ever participated makes the group suggestion system stand out in marked contrast to the individual suggestion system. The scanlon plan promoted cooperation, participation, and the sharing of information by both worker and management, as clearly indicated by Figures 4-2 and 4-3. Higher-quality suggestions are found under group suggestion systems since the acceptance rate of productivity-related suggestions is greater than under individual suggestion systems.

CHALLENGE TO MANAGEMENT

DeSoto also discovered that dealing with the scanlon plan over time provides management with both its greatest problem and challenge. The trial year is filled with much to learn, much excitement about this new organizational development, and much optimism about the bonus. However, time and familiarity diminish these factors significantly. Handling this situation as it occurs is a true sign of a successful firm. Successful plan firms such as DeSoto manage to rekindle the enthusiasm from that first year through a genuine interest in organizational development. Another factor that aids the firm in keeping the plan fresh is the natural relation of the bonus to the firm's ability to meet its markets effectively. No bonus accrues automatically. The bonus exists only if workers zealously pursue the goals of increasing quantity, improving quality, and reducing costs.

As seen in Figures 4-2 and 4-3, the number of suggestions can be expected to decline (given all other factors remain stable, i.e., economic conditions, technological developments, and organizational characteristics). At least two factors cause this situation. First, irritations in the work environment are being taken care of as productivity-related suggestion-making behavior is learned. Second, the potential for continued suggestion-making declines.

At DeSoto, four key roles emerge in support of the scanlon plan: (1) plant manager; (2) controller; (3) personnel manager; (4) departmental supervisor. Each of these roles has different duties, pressures, and opportunities that shape the quality of plan involvement and maintain this quality over time.

The most important role in the promotion and maintenance of the plan is the plant manager or chief executive officer. After 10 years of experience with scanlon, DeSoto Plant Manager Tom Lester has clearly demonstrated his expertise in performing the duties necessary to sustain the initial enthusiasm and vitality surrounding the plan. He has been a catalyst for successful and realistic goal setting and an ardent proponent of quality communication. Based on interviews with his workers, Tom Lester is viewed as a fair person and thus, he exemplifies a truly successful scanlon plant manager.

Another important role in promoting and maintaining the plan over time is that of the company controller. His role cannot be minimized. Jim Barker has more than adequately handled the ever-increasing responsibilities required of him under the plan. He frequently visits the production committee meetings and reviews their data. By doing this, he provides the workers with a constant reminder of high-cost areas that could be remedied by increased suggestion making. In this sense, Jim Barker is often viewed as the key to problem solving in the involvement system.

Another major role in the maintenance of the plan is the company personnel manager. His overall goal consists of communicating what scanlon is and what it is not to all levels of personnel. Bob Highland, personnel manager, has successfully achieved this goal. He provides orientation to all new personnel regarding the plan and notes plan activity that could be useful for future training and promotion decisions. More importantly, Bob Highland often serves as a reinforcer of the policy that affects the other roles previously discussed. In other words, he not only provides training and discussion for where DeSoto is but also, where DeSoto wants to be in the future.

DeSoto departmental supervisors occupy the fourth key role in maintaining successful operation of the plan over time. Besides the fact that many important decisions rest with them in terms of the acceptance or rejection of suggestions, departmental supervisors provide the essential link between management and workers. This link is necessary for the quality communication advocated by the scanlon philosophy. In this regard, the departmental supervisors play an indispensable role in the overall operation of the plan.

It takes more than these key people to successfully maintain or "feed" the program over time. DeSoto has developed task forces to stimulate the suggestion-making process. The task forces are formed at the departmental level and are given assignments. The information obtained from these assignments is then used for determining areas needing improvement and this information is later referred to the appropriate department.

Feeding the system requires good managers and workers that share their concerns, thoughts, and information on which production areas require attention. DeSoto obviously possesses such people and it is these people that make the entire revitalization of the plan successful.

INTANGIBLE BENEFITS OF THE PLAN AT DeSOTO

As mentioned earlier, the plan provides the organization with both tangible and intangible benefits. Following 10 years of experience and observations, DeSoto management across five scanlon plants were asked to cite the intangible benefits stemming from the incorporation of the scanlon philosophy into their organizations.

1. The plan provides the employees with the assurance that they will receive some degree of recognition by peers, by supervisors, and more importantly, by management. This is accomplished by the documentation and evaluation process required for all suggestions.
2. As stated previously, the plan increases the communication between all

employees within the organization through their participation in the involvement system.

3. Increased representation and variety of ideas are provided by the plan since management receives suggestions from all levels of employees.
4. Many suggestions result in savings to management in terms of time, training, and development. Examples of these are:
   a. Scanlon helps develop employees at all levels. This is done by workers actively participating in the involvement system and thus becoming better acquainted with the entire production process.
   b. The plan identifies employees with potential for supervisory or managerial positions. The production committees and screening committee provide a forum for the emergence and observation of leadership abilities.
   c. The plan educates employees regarding the need to justify capital budget requests. The mutual sharing of information and constant feedback on suggestions between management and workers provides the workers with management's rationale for accepting or rejecting suggestions.
   d. Where suggestions result in the addition of a capital item, the employees have a greater interest in getting the unit operating faster or overcoming start-up difficulties. Since the plan's emphasis on productivity improvement, the workers want the production process to run as smoothly as possible.
   e. As previously mentioned, workers become better acquainted with the entire production process through increased communication with all employees. This can contribute to a fresh approach to improving plant safety and housekeeping.
   f. Scanlon provides workers with the rationale for holding the total plant labor force to a minimum. Here again, this is the result of open communication between management and workers.
   g. The plan provides a means of uniting two or more departments in a common project. The involvement system and increased communication makes this situation possible.
   h. Finally, the plan is an important addition to the benefit package of the firm and provides the firm with a competitive advantage in the recruitment of new employees.

While tangible benefits are important in the assessment of the plan and its effect on the organization, the intangible benefits cannot and should not be ignored. They also influence productivity in a more subtle yet very important way. These benefits lend further support to the fact that the plan provides the organization and its workers with many advantages, thus making it a superior productivity improvement program.

SOCIAL–PSYCHOLOGICAL OUTCOMES OF THE PLAN

As previously mentioned, there are many consequences resulting from the plan. These consequences affect not only the organization as a whole but each individual employee as well. These social-psychological outcomes merit discussion in the fact that they add a more human quality to our discussion of scanlon at DeSoto. Also, by looking at employees' attitudes regarding the plan and its effect on the organization and on themselves, ideas for improvement and revitalization of the system are provided.

These outcomes were studied intensively over the 10-year period between 1971 and 1980. The attitudinal data were collected at different intervals during that time. The first took place during an 11-month period from October 1971 to August 1972. Seven years elapsed between the first survey and the data collected in July 1979. In 1971, there were 145 employees contacted. Of them, 142 (98%) agreed to participate in the survey. This group included managerial, clerical, and blue-collar personnel. The sales force was not included, as it lay outside the scope of the plan.

Later in 1971, each worker who had agreed to participate was contacted again after the plan was introduced but before a bonus was announced. Three months had elapsed. During this time, 6 individuals declined to participate and 17 were unavailable due to separation, illness, vacation, or military leave. This left 119 remaining in the survey group.

Very late in 1971, measures assessed the amount of learning based on communication and experience with the plan. Uniform questions with standard rating scales were carefully administered in face-to-face interviews. Comparisons of all three surveys use each individual's scores as his or her own control. In other words, any increase or decrease in knowledge of the plan or personal attitude toward the plan is measured by subtracting each person's score from his previous score on the same variable. Finally, in 1979, measurements were intended to evaluate workers' knowledge and attitudes regarding the plan over an extended period of time (eight years). Although this group was considerably smaller (18 people) than the last measurement group, 88%, or 16 individuals, in this measurement had participated in the three previous measurements. These attitudinal data were collected through informal group and single interviews occurring over a two-day period.

The social and psychological outcomes of the plan at the DeSoto plant can best be determined by first analyzing the data collected late in 1971 (approximately one year after plan installation) and then analyzing the data collected in 1979, (approximately eight years after plan installation). These two sets of data provide useful information in determining the short and long term effects of scanlon at DeSoto.

In 1971, the entire DeSoto population reflected high levels of general satisfaction with the plan. For example, over 90% of the employees expressed satisfaction with their employer "compared to most they know of." The blue-collar group, which is the main population for suggestion making, revealed that 77% of the DeSoto employees surveyed were satisfied with job security and 74% were satisfied with their pay.

It is interesting to note that many plan studies reveal initial low levels of employee satisfaction (including outright dissension—see Shultz, 1951).[5] This low level of satisfaction could be a reflection of skepticism on the part of the employee. Since the employee has had no prior experience with the plan, naturally he is skeptical about the possible benefits he and the organization could obtain from it.

However, late in 1971, this low level of satisfaction disappears and a significant increase in the satisfaction scores of the blue-collar group occurs. It should also be mentioned that interest in the job was found to be higher at this time, as was the feeling of accomplishment. These data also revealed an increase in scores in opportunity for being informed and an increase in scores in participation.

The literature of PG (Chapter 2) states that a major social and psychological outcome of the plan is the change in cooperation, participation, and communication; in other words, the nonbonus outcomes. Also, many experts have cited that the plan produces and enhances coordination and teamwork.[6,7,8,9]

These findings from previous research were substantiated at DeSoto. Opinions and attitudes about these social and psychological outcomes were elicited 1971. Table 4-2 reflects the net attitudinal change among both managerial and blue-collar workers across these two time periods. DeSoto managers were optimistic that participation might increase (some 90%). Later, all the company managers surveyed (100%) were certain that participation had increased.

In communication, 79% of the managers believed it might improve. Later (after eight months with the plan), 93% of the DeSoto managers felt communication had improved.

In the area of cooperation, the managers were less hopeful. Roughly 75% of the managers believed cooperation would improve under the plan. Later, this percentage remained the same, indicating that 75% of the managers felt cooperation had improved.

Overall, the blue-collar workers were more conservative in their estimates regarding increases in participation, communication, and cooperation. Early in 1971, only 44% of the blue-collar workers surveyed at DeSoto thought participation would increase. After eight months of experience with the plan, 82% perceived that participation had definitely improved.

Of DeSoto's blue-collar workers 65% believed that communication (both within departments and between departments) would improve with the plan. This perception increased only slightly later. At that time, 72% of the blue-collar workers thought that communication had improved.

Slightly more than half (53%) of the blue-collar workers believed that cooperation would be better under the plan. And 71% of the workers perceived a definite increase in cooperation.

Contrasting these two groups (managers and blue-collar workers) is essential for understanding the true impact of the plan on all employees. As is clearly evidenced by the change in attitudinal data, DeSoto managers were higher in their perceptions of the plan and its effect on participation, communication, and cooperation than the blue-collar workers. This perceptual difference between the two groups of employees could possibly be the result of increased familiarity and understanding of the plan on the part of DeSoto managers. Also, the fact that it was explained to the managers how important it was for them to be supportive of the plan in order for it to be successful could have caused the higher perceptions on the part of the managers. It should be remembered, however, that although the blue-collar workers were more conservative in their opinions about these factors, their net attitudinal change was in a positive direction.

Up until now, our discussion has focused on the short-term effects of the plan at DeSoto. While the net changes spanning the first year experience are impressive, the ultimate question at the end of that first year was, Could these nonbonus outcomes keep improving? In 1979, data provided the answer to this question.

Looking at survey data collected in 1979 is instructional. Again, we will divide our analysis into two groups—managers and blue-collar workers. In terms of participation, 100% of DeSoto managers surveyed believed participation, had increased within the first year of the plan's inception. In 1979, only 67% of the managers felt that participation had improved since the trial year's increase. This decrease has numerous implications and possible explanations.

The most obvious explanation is that participation had, in fact, declined. It is important to note, at this time, that most DeSoto employees (managers and blue-collar workers) surveyed were using the number of suggestions made as a measure of participation. This fact leads to a second possible explanation for the decrease in perceived participation on the part of DeSoto managers. The number of suggestions made may not be an accurate measure of participation. Therefore, a decrease in suggestion making over the years does not necessarily mean a decrease in participation. Suggestions could decrease for several reasons. Possibly the ideas or reasons for suggestions have dried up or people are making suggestions without using the formal suggestion-making procedure, which would result in suggestions not getting reported. So, the decline in perceived levels of participation does not necessarily signify a decline in actual employee participation.

In the area of communication, 89% of DeSoto's managers felt that communication had improved over the years. This percentage represented a 4% decrease since the 1971 data collection. This decrease can be attributed to the addition of one new manager to our survey who was not familiar enough with the plan to determine any significant change in communication one way or the other.

Regarding cooperation, once again 89% of DeSoto's managers surveyed believed cooperation had improved. This is significant perceptual change (+ 12%) from 1971.

DeSoto's blue-collar workers were also questioned to determine their attitudes concerning changes in participation, communication, and cooperation over the eight-year period. With respect to participation, 63% of the blue-collar workers observed an increase in participation levels. This represents a 19% decline from the 1971 data collection. The same reasons mentioned for the managers' decline in perceived levels of participation could also apply to the blue-collar workers.

Of the blue-collar workers surveyed at DeSoto 88% believed communication had improved since 1971. This percentage represents a 16% increase over the time span between 1971 and 1979.

Regarding cooperation, 88% of the blue-collar workers perceived an improvement in cooperation by 1979. A 17% increase from 1971 is signified by this percentage. An important point to remember is that the blue-collar workers exhibited initially low levels of optimism regarding the chance for improvements in participation, communication, and cooperation. These significant increases in perceived improvements in communication and cooperation could be the result of the blue-collar workers' initial conservative feeling about the plan.

Overall, the social and psychological outcomes of the plan at DeSoto can be classified as positive. However, these positive outcomes are not assured by the plan. In other words, the success of the plan is determined by many factors—some under the control of DeSoto management and some not. Those factors that helped determine the success of the plan were: (1) a clear understanding of the plan and how it works by all employees; (2) a supportive and optimistic attitude by all personnel in critical roles in the organization (managers and first-line supervisors); and (3) an overall organizational climate of acceptance and trust.

The first factor was felt to be under management's control. The presentation of the plan is crucial to its successful operation. Therefore, DeSoto management paid close attention to the methodology used to introduce and familiarize the workforce with the plan since it realized the effects would be felt for years to come.

The second factor was partially under management's control but was also dependent on the type of personality found in the organization's key roles. While all personnel in critical roles may appear supportive and optimistic, it is still possible for these key people to seriously undermine the plan. If these key people are unsure of their own abilities, autocratic in their interpersonal relationships, or threatened by change, their surface support and optimism will soon be detected. Then, the plan may appear manipulative and spurious. So, it is imperative that all management be genuinely supportive of the plan in order to ensure its success. DeSoto had only minor problems in this regard.

The third and final factor is also partially under the control of management but is also influenced by the personalities found in the workforce. Management can and should counsel and reassure workers. This will help promote and foster a climate of both acceptance and trust. However, management does not solely influence the organizational climate. The success and, in a sense, the foundation of the plan rests on the workforce made up of individuals who fit the following profile. These people should be

1. high on interpersonal trust measures;
2. reinforced and motivated by group beliefs rather than individual beliefs;
3. motivated by extrinsic factors rather than intrinsic factors, i.e., pay for productivity.

It is not mandatory that all workers fit this profile, but a majority of the DeSoto workforce did. If this is not the case, the goals of increasing participation, communication, and cooperation can never be achieved.

In summary, an in-depth analysis supports several conclusions. Looking at the data on both a short- and long-term basis, it is clear that managers and subordinates view the plan differently. Possible reasons for this were discussed. However, these perceptual differences, as represented in Table 4–2, appear to be stable over time. Finally, factors affecting the success or failure of the plan were discussed. Overall, after 10 years' experience with the plan, levels of trust and satisfaction are high as are perceived levels of participation, communication, and cooperation. There appears to be no reason why all these outcomes will not continue at DeSoto.

CONCLUSIONS

Productivity at DeSoto appears to be enhanced by the plan. The bonus formula, which measures productivity, shows an average payroll bonus of 7.8% over the years. When this result is combined with a careful accounting of units of output, labor costs, and hours worked, the gains to productivity are high—as high as 52%.

Construction and maintenance of the bonus formula over time raises special problems in fostering an atmosphere of equity and mutual trust. It is often necessary to change the formula because of external demand and pricing factors. Some workers do not understand this and they then see the plan as manipulative. The decision to use a simple rather than comprehensive bonus formula depends on the complexity of the organization and how important worker understanding of the formula is to management.

The analysis of the involvement system at DeSoto reveals that irritants with the working environment are a common source of suggestions in the early stages of the plan. However, as learning occurs, productivity-related suggestions dominate—especially those that focus on quantity. Productivity also affects suggestion-making behavior. Slack-period suggestions reflect ideas not related to productivity. Feeding the system with accounting and technical information is especially helpful in overcoming this problem.

Costs associated with operating the plan, such as time spent in meetings, appear to be outweighed by the benefits, both tangible and intangible. Indeed, the benefits of the plan appear to be the reason it has remained viable through the years at DeSoto. Also, numerous studies have indicated that the quality of the national labor force is constantly improving. As this occurs, the industrial culture becomes more conducive to this form of sharing information in order to improve productivity.

Finally, the installation and maintenance of the plan required DeSoto management to consider a number of key issues. Based on the available information and the result of management's evaluation, the following recommendations were made. It is important to note that these recommendations are not unique to DeSoto. Therefore, they might be applied to any firm contemplating using the plan.

1. Key people in managerial and working ranks should possess a thorough understanding of the formula and filter this knowledge to others in the organization. These people should be identified and exposed to the mechanics of the formula early on in the formulation and installation process. Good distribution and circulation of these individuals enhance employee acceptance and trust in the plan.

2. Complaints or dissatisfiers in the work environment have been shown to be the most common suggestion type received initially. Managers should anticipate these nonproductive suggestions in such a way as to (a) instruct production committees that these suggestions will have no effect on the bonus and (b) deal with the substance of the nonproductive suggestion by encouraging union leadership to handle them. If no union exists, then management must still deal with the nonproductive suggestions on a basis perceived to be outside the plan. Some of the nonproductive suggestions may be processed as suggestions, i.e., accepted and implemented. These suggestions should be reviewed at a later time as nonproductivity-related suggestions and be processed (in terms of policy) outside of the plan.

3. Another suggestion related issue is the decline of suggestions over time. All organizational leaders should actively seek out opportunities to "feed the system" and direct efforts toward new areas. One role in the organization keenly suited for this task is the controller or chief cost accountant. By participating in production committee meetings, he can indicate high-cost services or operations, inform the committee of redundancies in services or operations or point out cyclical costs with the objective of smoothing the production process.

4. Front-line supervisors may feel threatened by new types of participation and high rates of suggestions from their departments (including grievances). Managers and consultants must work with the supervisors by counseling and reassuring them. There may be some turnover at this level of supervision but the suggestion system can help solve this problem by identifying promotable individuals.

5. All information should be provided so that they perceive a definite and causal link between behaviors and rewards. Committee meetings can and should be utilized to transmit this information.

6. Since individuals differ in the ability to communicate information, it is often necessary to individualize communication regarding the plan. That is, the communication must be tailored to the ability of the employee to receive the information. Again, the committee system can facilitate this end.

7. Finally, frequently the plan is presented as a structure or formula that will produce greater cooperation and productivity. This emphasis ignores the process of participation. Basic human values and attitudes about work, co-workers, the organization, and our economic system are at stake. Therefore, DeSoto management believes that there is no substitute for organizational policies built on trust and mutual dependence. The process of participation can be enhanced by supportive training in interpersonal skills for all organizational members. This type of training helps smooth the process of group interaction so basic to the plan's success.

DeSoto (Garland) has its scanlon plan 12 years at this writing. The ensuing years have brought many changes to the people of DeSoto. However, the plan is still alive and vital to the interests of all concerned. It has accomplished the original goals of Tom Lester, while introducing many new objectives worthy of pursuit. Solely for its value as a communication system, DeSoto management would keep the plan. As a way of life at the workplace, however, it appears that the entire workforce wishes to keep the plan.

NOTES

1. Brian E. Moore, *A Plant-Wide Productivity Plan in Action: Three Years of Experience with the Scanlon Plan*, (Washington, D.C.: National Commission on Productivity and Work Quality, 1975).

2. Brian E. Moore and Timothy L. Ross, *The Scanlon Way to Improved Productivity* (New York: Wiley-Interscience, 1978).

3. Carl F. Frost, J.H. Wakely, and R.A. Ruh, *The Scanlon Plan for Organization Development: Identity, Participation, Equity* (East Lansing: Michigan State University Press, 1974).

4. Robert B. McKersie, "Wage Payment Methods of the Future," *British Journal of Industrial Relations*, June 1963, pp. 191–212.

5. George P. Shultz, "Worker Participation on Production Problems," *Personnel*, November 1951, 209–11.

6. Frost et al., *The Scanlon Plan for Organization Development*.

7. Frederick G. Lesieur, ed., *The Scanlon Plan—A Frontier in Labor-Management Cooperation* (Cambridge: Technology Press of M.I.T. and New York: Wiley, 1958).

8. Robert B. McKersie, "Wage Payment Methods of the Future," *British Journal of Industrial Relations*, June 1963, pp. 191–212.

9. Joseph N. Scanlon, "Talk on Union Management Relations" (Proceedings on Conference Productivity, Industrial Relations Center, University of Wisconsin, 1949) pp. 10–18.

5

Improshare:
The Fastest Growing
PG Plan in the 1980s

by Brian E. Graham-Moore

Without question, Improshare has gained wide acceptance by many American manufacturing concerns. More than 100 Improshare plans have been installed since 1976. As we mentioned in Chapter 2, Improshare is the brainchild of Mitchell Fein, engineer, educator, and consultant. His first written materials on PG date to 1971.[1] At that time Fein was establishing ceiling and buy-back principles for wage incentive plans. Improshare itself is based on work standards extended to cover the entire plant. Indeed, Fein's breakthrough came by selectively editing the soundest part of productivity measurement (time standards) and using it in aggregate form for his version of PG.

In his paper "Establishing Time Standards By Parameters,"[2] Fein lays out the principles for traditional bases for work measurement. He then builds on these principles to include measurements of two types: (1) historical and (2) co-variation of indirect with direct (where measurement exists).

Let us pursue the historical measurement as this is a departure from traditional work measurement techniques (e.g., stopwatch time study). As Fein states:[3]

> Measurement by parameters sets standards at the average of the past, using historical data within a place of work, with no need to performance rate the work performance data. The rationale for this

TABLE 5-1 Improshare Experience

Firm	Industry	Technology	# Employees	Coverage	Date	Reported Bonus Range or Average	Status
1. Hinderliter Energy Equipment Corporation Tulsa, Oklahoma	Mfg. of tubing and forgings	Mass/unit, small and centralized	320	All shop employees	1978	1–23%	Positive: shipping 25% more product after plan, turnover cut in half
2. Columbus Auto Parts Columbus, Ohio	Mfg. of auto and truck front end parts	Capital intensive decentralized	815	Plantwide	1979	0–17%	Positive: despite many market problems of the auto industry, workers elected to keep the plan
3. Presto-Lite (Oklahoma Plant)	Mfg. of DC motors	Mass/unit, small, decentralized	320	Plantwide	1978	7–14%	Positive: an involvement system installed with Improshare is a success
4. R.M. Friction Materials Crawfordsville, Indiana	Mfg. of clutch and brake blocks	Batch, small decentralized	100	Plantwide	1976	0–50%	Positive: productivity matches bonus
5. Coast Catamaran (Division of Coleman) Irvine, California	Mfg. of catamarans ("Hobie Cats")	Mass/unit, small, decentralized	200	Plantwide	1978	"Average of 10%"	Positive: growth of production and markets will increase coverage of Improshare to larger unit. Productivity gains measured at 20%
6. Hackney and Sons (East) Inc. Hamilton, Ontario	Mfg. of beverage truck bodies	Low technology, batch	470	Plantwide across two plants	1976	8–30%	Positive: productivity has risen to 105% and 140% in the two plants. Turnover has been reduced by a factor of 6.
7. Champion Container Division (formerly Hoerner-Waldorf) San Francisco, California	Mfg. of paper containers	—	—	—	1975	—	Several other locations have installed the plan, thus this experience appears positive

Company / Location	Description	Process	Employees	Scope	Year		Results
8. Corry Jamestown Corporation Corry, Pennsylvania	Mfg. of metal office furniture	Batch, small	700	Plantwide across two plants	1978	—	Positive: 40% increase in productivity reported
9. Rockwell-Texarkana Texarkana, Arkansas	Mfg. of pipe clamps and couplings	—	200	Plantwide	1979	—	—
10. Firestone Canada, Inc. Hamilton, Ontario	Mfg. of tires	Mass/unit, large	1,550	Plantwide	1980	—	—
11. International Steel Evansville, Indiana	Mfg. of structural steel products	Batch	377	Plantwide	1980	—	—
12. The Norton Company Huntsville, Alabama	Mfg. of abrasive products	—	—	—	1977	—	Positive: average productivity gain of 19% per-year. Four other plants received the plan.
13. Atlas Powder Company Subsidiary of Tyler Corp. Dallas, Texas	—	—	675	Plantwide across two plants	—	—	—
14. McGraw-Edison* Cambridge, Ontario (*Now, Canadian Admiral)	Mfg. of home appliances	Mass/unit, large	400	Plantwide	1979	—	Positive: labor relations improved. Productivity up by 20%
15. Mead Paper Printing & Writing Division Kingsport, Tennessee	Mfg. of home appliances	Continuous process	1,000	Plantwide	1979	—	—
16. Hickory Manufacturing Company Hickory, North Carolina	Mfg. of furniture	Continuous process	1,000	Plant employees only	1980	—	Positive: productivity up by 15%
17. Tell City Chair Company Tell City, Indiana	Mfg. of chair seats	Mass/unit, small	25	One dept.	1978	—	Positive: the company plans to phase out other incentives in favor of Improshare
18. Peterson Industries Freedonia, Wisconsin	Mfg. or metal stampings	Batch, small	90	Plantwide	1978	—	Positive: productivity up by 30%
19. Tube Manufacturing Company Somerville, New Jersey	Mfg. of rolled welded tube	Continuous process	35	Hourly Workers	1978	—	Positive: productivity up 25% per year

approach is that "yesterday's performance is established as the Accepted Productivity Level (APL). Measurements tomorrow will be made against this APL base.

Fein elaborates a technique that is different from traditional stopwatch measurement and very similar to some of the other PG formulas described in Moore and Ross and referenced in Chapter 2 and 3.[4] However, the significant difference between Improshare and all other PG formulas is the conversion of the key components of productivity measurements into time standards. Most other PG formulas use the ratio of labor dollars to sales dollar (see Table 3-1).

In addition, most other PG plans involve the entire firm. Improshare may measure part of a firm, but usually covers the entire company. The formula uses man-hours of labor input compared with the man-hour output value of finished goods. It is Fein's contention that "measuring by hours produced by product, compared to hours worked by all employees, eliminates the influence of product mix and market changes [1980, personal correspondence]." There is little question that this formula achieves this goal. However, the rapid acceptance of Improshare is due to many factors—not just a formula that is less sensitive to market changes and fluctuating materials costs.

Some of these factors are the traditional ones that have always influenced the PG-oriented firm, in this case the Improshare firm. For example:

1. Plantwide sharing of bonuses increases cooperation.
2. Increased productivity of the firm is shared by participating employees.
3. Goals of productivity are perceived as attainable.
4. Trust between management and worker is sufficiently high to warrant an "innovation."
5. The time is ripe to move away from narrow interests in favor of rewarding as many as possible for gains in labor productivity.

The factors that are particular to Improshare cause some speculation. For example, a partial listing of firms that are using Improshare can be found in Table 5-1. All of these firms are manufacturers (yet Improshare can work in service organizations). These manufacturers range from small (100) to large (1,550). Technology of these firms ranges from semiskilled, batch process to high skill and also mass process. These firms use Improshare plantwide most often. That is, the bonus touches the lives of virtually everyone. Some firms use Improshare for shop employees only, and, conceivably, some could use it only for one class of employee or for one or two departments. Overall, the firms where information exists, as reflected in Table 5-1, suggest that the initial impact of Improshare on productivity has been good.

Since most PG plans are started by managers, it may be that those firms with confidence in standard time measures and "traditional" industrial engineering measurements are drawn to the Improshare formula. Since managers won't recommend incentive formulas they don't fully understand, this may be one clue as to why Improshare has taken off.

Nevertheless, many firms with no background in time standards are experimenting with Improshare. This is probably due to the prodigious contribution to the management and PG literature by Mitchell Fein.[5,6,7,8,9,10] Fein has also lectured at the Wharton Business School for many years. Interestingly, most of the PG literature has centered on the scanlon plan (see Chapter 2). Since 1971, however, Fein has contributed a number of serious, scholarly papers that lay the groundwork for Improshare. These articles have provided more explanation of components of Improshare than many of the more numerous scanlon case studies.

Finally, where does Improshare fit in the domain of PG? As the reader will recall in Chapter 1, Improshare doesn't have the philosophical underpinnings of scanlonism. Improshare can be packaged to portions of the firm while the scanlon plan rarely, if ever, is. Improshare does have constraints, such as the ceiling and buy back provisions, which serve to put limits on the bonus payout. Improshare may or may not have an involvement system.

For many reasons such as these, we have classed Improshare as an initial, evolutionary step in PG development (see Figure 1-2). However, depending on how Improshare is packaged, it could represent PG as the highest level. That is, Improshare with all employees included and with an involvement system could be PG as a way of life.

NOTES

1. Mitchell Fein, "Wage Incentive Plans," in *Industrial Engineering Handbook*, ed. H.B. Maynard, 3rd ed. (New York: McGraw-Hill Book Company, 1971) pp. 6–33.

2. ——, "Establishing Time Standard Parameters," in *Proceedings of the American Institute of Industrial Engineers*, Annual Conference, Spring 1978.

3. Ibid.

4. Brian E. Moore, *Sharing the Gains of Productivity* (Scarsdale, N.Y.: Work in America Institute Studies in Productivity, 1982).

5. Fein, "Wage Incentive Plans."

6. ———, "The Real Needs and Goals of Blue Collar Workers," *The Conference Board Record*, February 1973.

7. ———, "Improving Productivity by Improved Productivity Sharing," *Conference Board Record*, July 1976, pp. 44–49.

8. ———, "Establishing Time Standard Parameters."

9. ———, "An Alternative to Traditional Managing," in *Handbook of Industrial Engineering*, ed. Gavriel Salvendy (New York: Wiley, 1982).

10. ———, "Financial Motivation," in *Handbook of Industrial Engineering*, ed. Gavriel Salvendy (New York: Wiley, 1982), Chapter 23.

6

PG and the Construction Industry: A Delphi Study

by Alexander Laufer

Construction productivity, far from ever being optimal, has steadily declined over the last 10 years.[1,2] With construction constituting about 10% of the U.S. GNP and also being so labor-intensive, this industry is a deserving target of investigation for ways to improve labor efficiency. A common method other industries use to improve labor efficiency is the financial incentive program (FIP).[3,4] The construction industry in the U.S. has, with negligible exceptions, failed to adopt some form of incentive program to further its productivity.

Construction industries in certain foreign countries, on the other hand, have effectively employed financial incentive programs.[5,6,7] Marriott reports studies in England comparing construction labor expenditure under fixed-wage payments and incentive payments.[8] The results showed that the change to the incentive pay program resulted in a saving of 15% of manhours. Another study shows that the average level of output achieved after introducing a financial incentive program was 34% above the previous level.[9]

The example set by foreign countries justifies a thorough inquiry into the possibilities of applying incentive programs in the U.S. construction industry. This study attempts to determine: (1) the causes for the low incidence of financial incentive programs in the U.S. construction industry; (2) the attitudes of the involved parties toward the introduction of the programs and how they can be favorably influenced; and (3) the prevalence and effectiveness of the various managerial approaches to motivation. Another part of the study is devoted to evaluating various methods for measuring on-site performance and predicting the effectiveness of different financial incentive programs. A complete presentation of the findings of the study is included in its final report.[10]

RESEARCH METHODOLOGY

Data Gathering Procedure

The Delphi technique was used to obtain the answers to the preceding questions. This is a method of eliciting and refining group judgments. The Delphi technique can be described as an exercise in which a small monitor team designs a questionnaire that is sent to a larger respondent group. After the questionnaire is returned, the monitor team summarizes the results and, based upon the results, develops a new questionnaire for the respondent group. The respondent group is usually given at least one opportunity to reevaluate its original answers based upon the examination of the group response.[11,12]

The Delphi panel in this study included 37 specialists of various interrelated professions such as contractors, owners, (clients), union officials, university professors, and productivity consultants. The study comprised three rounds of questionnaires of which two included feedback of results.

The breakdown of the participation by sectors of respondents is shown in Table 6-1. The 37 participants were from 19 states across the U.S. and represented some of the most respected authorities in construction.

Analysis and Presentation of the Results

The nature of the question and the distribution of the results determined the method of presenting the answers. The methods were:

a. Percentages.
b. Percentages and Midpoint Response (MPR). The MPR is the point above and below which 50% of the response lies.
c. Midpoint Response and Interquartile Range (IQR). The IQR is the interval containing the middle 50% of the responses.

For the analysis of some of the questions during the Delphi sequence the responses of the participants were grouped according to their occupations as follows: contractors, owners, professors and productivity consultants,

TABLE 6-1   Participation and Returns by Group of Respondents

GROUP (1)	INVITED (2)	AGREED TO PARTICIPATE (3)	COMPLETED ROUND 1 (4)	COMPLETED ROUND 2 (5)	COMPLETED ROUND 3 (6)
Contractors	17	14	12	10	9
Owners	10	7	7	6	6
Professors	11	10	8	7	7
Consultants	7	6	6	4	4
Union officials	12	5	4	4	4
Total	57	42	37	31	30

and union officials. It was found, however, that the MPR of the 4 groups were very close on most issues.

An attempt to group the participants according to the type of construction they represented (i.e., building, heavy, or industrial) resulted generally in higher dispersion of response. Another attempt to divide the panelists into more homogeneous groups consisting of members of the same occupation and the same type of construction, was meaningless because of the very small size of these groups. The dispersion of results within these minigroups was of the same magnitude as within the larger groups. For these reasons most of the results in the final analysis were tabulated and presented for the panel as a whole. References were made to significantly deviating groups.

LOW INCIDENCE OF FINANCIAL INCENTIVE PROGRAMS

The causes of the low incidence of financial incentive programs in construction in the U.S. are debatable. The traditional controversy is whether the low incidence of the programs is due to the construction environment, to the variable nature of the work and the conditions under which it takes place, or to managerial deficiencies. Arguing that the low incidence is due to problems endemic to the industry's operations would in fact provide the answer to the central question of this study, to wit, that financial incentive programs are not feasible in the construction industry. The findings clearly demonstrate that though some difficulties of implementing certain types of financial incentive programs stem from the specific nature of construction, the panel did not regard them as the major obstacles but believed in the feasibility of employing such programs in the construction industry.

According to the panel the low incidence is due to

1. tradition and conservatism of the industry;
2. the nature of the work; and
3. union opposition.

Typical causes related to tradition and conservatism are

1. lack of experience with FIP;
2. the general unwillingness of the industry to try new radical approaches; and
3. the absence of proven success with FIP.

Common causes stemming from the specific nature of construction are

1. the difficulty of establishing standards for all possible circumstances;
2. the difficulty in measuring output because of the mixture of quantity and quality; and
3. the significant variations in the working conditions over which the worker has no control.

The union opposition toward FIP is discussed in the following section.

The extent to which the lack of financial incentive programs is due to managerial deficiencies was explored in depth. The findings are most interesting. On the one hand good management is deemed essential for the success of the programs; on the other hand implementation of the programs would result in a better management. As for the present quality of management, a small majority of the experts expressed the belief that the chances that management would benefit from the programs are higher than the failure risks imposed on the program by poor management. The beneficiary effects on the quality of management will be due to: (1) work study associated with FIP that will directly stimulate everyone to improve the organization of the job and eliminate inefficiency and waste; (2) refinement in job performance measurement; and (3) labor pressure for continuity of work.

ATTITUDE TOWARD FINANCIAL INCENTIVE PROGRAMS

Construction of the Questions

The questions in this section were based on a list of 38 statements delineating some of the effects, positive and negative, that financial incentive programs might have on the various factors of the work. The 38 effects were divided into 15 groups. The effects within each group were related to one factor of the work. For example, the work factor "peer relations" could be affected in the following ways: (1) Workers might be encouraged to work as a team for their personal benefit, or (2) Jealousies might arise among the workers because some are able to earn more than others, or because fast workers will be dissatisfied with the slower or older workers in the group. The questions that were referred to the parties involved the introduction of financial incentive programs: contractors, employees, union officials, and owners (clients). The panel was asked to examine how the effects that financial incentive programs might have on each aspect will influence the attitude of each party toward the introduction of the programs.

The answers were given on a seven-point scale from (1) Very Opposed through (4) Neutral to (7) Very Supportive. Each aspect was studied independently. The panelist was to decide which effect, positive or negative, would be perceived as dominant by the party under investigation. If the positive effect was perceived as dominant, the level of support expected from that party depended on the intensity of the effect and importance of the aspect. The same principle determined the level of opposition if the negative effect was perceived as dominant. The lower the intensity of the effect and the lower the importance of the aspect the closer the answer was to neutral.

The Attitude of the Contractors

Most panelists believed that there were no effects of sufficient weight to induce opposition to FIP by contractors. In fact, the MPR was positive on 11 factors, and neutral on the remaining 4. Only in regard to 5 factors the IQR scored within a negative range. (See Figure 6-1.)

The effects of financial incentive programs on four factors—total productivity, quantity of production, production cost, and methods improvements—will render the contractors supportive. Three other factors—recruitment, workers' satisfaction, and execution of work—will dispose the contractors to be somewhat supportive. In all of the above factors the level of agreement among the participants was high. At least 50% of the responses converged on two points of the seven-point scale, and at least 75% viewed the contractors as supportive. Regarding safety, contractors were presumed to be somewhat supportive but there was less agreement among the participants. An MPR of 5 was also given to management sophistication and management-worker relations with an even larger divergence. In both aspects the contractors expected their colleagues (the contractor party) to be more in favor of the introduction than viewed by the rest of the panel.

The Attitude of the Employees

The employees were assumed to be supportive of the introduction of FIPs because of their effects on five work factors, to be neutral because of the effects on eight work factors, and opposed because of two factors (Figure 6-2).

The majority of the participants agreed that the employees will be

FIGURE 6-1 Contractors' Attitudes to Incentives

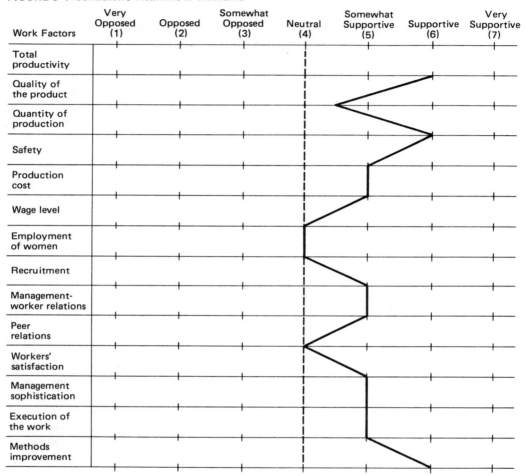

Work Factors	Very Opposed (1)	Opposed (2)	Somewhat Opposed (3)	Neutral (4)	Somewhat Supportive (5)	Supportive (6)	Very Supportive (7)
Total productivity							
Quality of the product							
Quantity of production							
Safety							
Production cost							
Wage level							
Employment of women							
Recruitment							
Management-worker relations							
Peer relations							
Workers' satisfaction							
Management sophistication							
Execution of the work							
Methods improvement							

supportive, because of the effects on wage level and the effect on workers' satisfaction, and somewhat supportive because of the total productivity factor. The employees were also viewed as somewhat supportive because of quantity of production, with the exception of most owners, who did not share this view. The MPR on safety was 4.5, but the responses were widely dispersed.

There was a high consensus of opinion as to the neutral attitude of the employees as a result of the effect on production cost, employment of women and management sophistication. Though all groups agreed that the employee's attitude will be neutral due to the effect on quality of the product, management-worker relations and execution of the work, there was less agreement among the individual participants. The MPR for recruitment was 4, yet many of the professor-consultant group rated it negative.

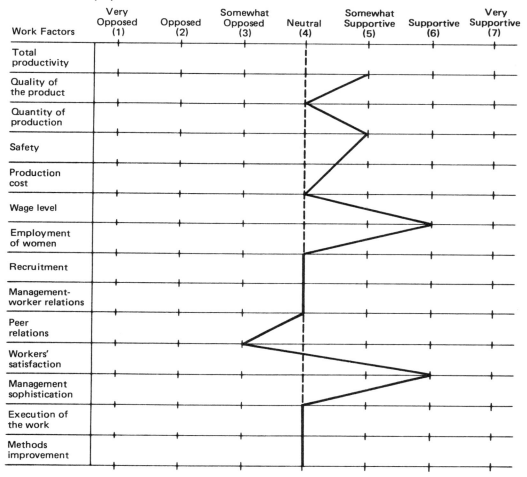

FIGURE 6-2 Employees' Attitudes to Incentives

The MPR for Methods improvement was also 4, though many of the contractors and owners gave a negative rating.

All the groups perceived the employees as somewhat opposed to the introduction of FIP because of their possible effect on employment and peer relations.

The Attitude of the Union Officials

Union officials were perceived as opposed to the introduction of FIP because of their effect on seven factors of the work, as neutral because of the effect on six work factors, and as supportive due to two factors (Figure 6-3).

All groups agreed that the unions' strongest opposition will be due

101

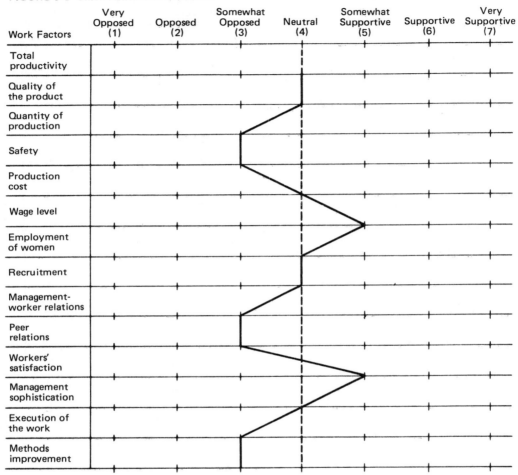

FIGURE 6-3 Union Attitude to Incentives

Work Factors	Very Opposed (1)	Opposed (2)	Somewhat Opposed (3)	Neutral (4)	Somewhat Supportive (5)	Supportive (6)	Very Supportive (7)
Total productivity							
Quality of the product							
Quantity of production							
Safety							
Production cost							
Wage level							
Employment of women							
Recruitment							
Management-worker relations							
Peer relations							
Workers' satisfaction							
Management sophistication							
Execution of the work							
Methods improvement							

to the effect on employment. Most of the participants in each of the three panel groups agreed that union officials will be somewhat opposed because of the effect on quantity of production, management-worker relations, peer relations, execution of the work, and methods improvement. Though union officials were also considered somewhat opposed because of the effect on safety, there was a wide dispersion of opinion within all groups.

The MPR for total productivity and quality of the product was 4. Though the MPR for production cost, employment of women, recruitment, and management sophistication was also 4, the majority ranked them negative.

All groups expected union officials to be somewhat supportive because of the effect on workers' satisfactions. Though the majority also

102

held that union officials will be somewhat supportive because of the effect on wage level, opinions between contractors and owners were polarized, the former perceiving them as opposed and the latter as supportive.

The Attitude of the Owners

Most of the panelists presumed owners to be supportive because of the effect on eight work factors and neutral because of the effect on the other seven (Figure 6-4).

The MPR for total productivity, quantity of production, and production cost was 6. The MPR for management-worker relations, worker satisfaction, management sophistication, execution of the work, and

FIGURE 6-4 Owners' Attitudes to Incentives

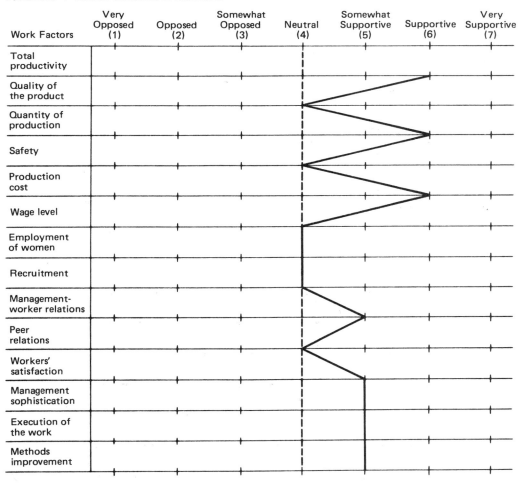

methods improvement was 5. For all eight aspects consensus of opinion was high. Many respondents presumed owners to have a neutral attitude because of the effect on employment, employment of women, recruitment and peer relations. Among those who did not perceive the attitude as neutral, more perceived them as supportive than as opposed.

Comparison Between the Parties

It is difficult to make a quantitative comparison between the attitudes of the various parties mainly because the relative importance of each aspect is not known and because it is most probably different for each party. Nevertheless, to obtain a general indication of the overall attitude of each party the mean of the MPRs for all aspects was calculated. For this purpose the 1 to 7 rating scale was transformed into a -3 to +3 scale, 0 thus expressing neutral. The mean MPR in descending order were as follows: contractors = +0.90, owners = +0.73, employees = +0.30, and union officials = -0.40. The overall attitude of the parties is also reflected in Figure 6-5. In all but three factors—production cost, wage level, and workers satisfaction—no party scored a higher MPR than contractors. In all but three factors, "wage level," "employment of women," and "workers satisfaction," no party scored a lower MPR than union officials.

Contractors and owners were perceived to have common attitudes (Figure 6-5). In 10 factors their MPRs were identical, and in the remaining the difference between the MPRs was not larger than 1.

Out of the 15 factors the MPRs of union officials and employees were equal only in 6, while in all other factors employees were perceived to be more in favor than union officials.

What Will Improve the Attitude
of the Parties?

The answers to the preceding question places one in a position to determine which effects of the programs will bias the parties strongest against the introduction of FIP. To improve the attitude of the parties one should first concentrate on eliminating the negative affects. The investigation included only the three parties represented in the panel: the contractors, the owners, and the union officials.

The most common remedies offered to neutralize the opposition of the parties were to publicize successful programs employed elsewhere and to embark on a variety of research projects. Specific suggestions referred to either the financial incentive programs proper or to the existing control systems. For instance, it was suggested to modify the programs so that quality and safety would also be embraced. On the other hand, recommendations were put forward to improve the existing quality control

FIGURE 6-5 Combined Attitudes of Contractors, Owners, Employees, and Unions

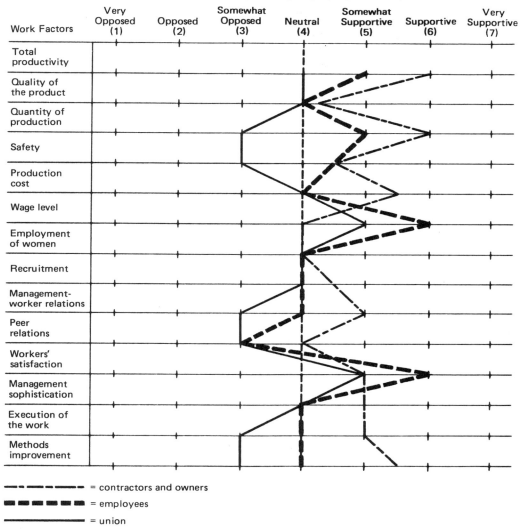

Work Factors	Very Opposed (1)	Opposed (2)	Somewhat Opposed (3)	Neutral (4)	Somewhat Supportive (5)	Supportive (6)	Very Supportive (7)
Total productivity							
Quality of the product							
Quantity of production							
Safety							
Production cost							
Wage level							
Employment of women							
Recruitment							
Management-worker relations							
Peer relations							
Workers' satisfaction							
Management sophistication							
Execution of the work							
Methods improvement							

— - — - — - — - — = contractors and owners

▬ ▬ ▬ ▬ ▬ ▬ = employees

——————————— = union

and assurance systems and the accident prevention programs without linkage to FIP.

Sharing the costs of introducing and administering the programs between the contractor and the owner or between the contractor and the employees or between several contractors was offered as a means to reduce the financial risks involved in the introduction of the programs. Providing adequate training in the administration of FIP to both private consultants and construction managers was another common suggestion. A third suggestion supported by many was to simplify the programs to ease their administration. This recommendation is often stressed in the literature but mainly in order to ensure the employees' understanding.

Of the steps recommended by the panel to reduce the opposition of the union, the most prominent one was to involve the union in the design of the programs and in setting the standards. The only way to alleviate the unions' strongest objection—the threat of unemployment—would be to communicate that greater productivity would eventually lead to more work.

CONSTRUCTION MANAGERS' APPROACHES TO MOTIVATION

Laufer[13] showed that one of the major factors affecting decisions concerning new pay practices is management approach to motivation. A common model identifies three patterns of managerial approaches to motivation.[14]

The first, termed the traditional approach, assumes that: (1) work is inherently distasteful to most people; (2) workers care less about what they do than about what they earn for doing it; and (3) only few workers want or handle work that requires creativity, self-direction, or self-control.

The second approach, the human relations approach, argues that: (1) people want to feel useful and important; (2) people desire to belong and to be recognized as individuals; and (3) these needs are more important than money in motivating people to work. The basic goal in both the traditional and the human relations approaches is much the same, aiming at securing employee compliance with managerial authority.

Finally, the human resources approach assumes that: (1) people want to contribute on the job; (2) work does not necessarily have to be distasteful; and (3) employees are quite capable of making significant and rational decisions affecting their work, and allowing greater latitude in employee decision making is in the best interest of the organization.

The panelists were presented with the policies of the three managerial approaches as follows:

Traditional Approach
1. The manager's basic task is to closely supervise and control subordinates.
2. The manager must break tasks down into simple, repetitive, easily learned operations.
3. The manager must establish detailed work routines and procedures and enforce these firmly but fairly.

Human Relations Approach

1. The manager's basic task is to make each worker feel useful and important.
2. The manager should keep subordinates informed and listen to their objections to his or her plans.
3. The manager should allow subordinates to exercise some self-direction and self-control on routine matters.

Human Resources Approach

1. The manager's basic task is to make use of "untapped" human resources.
2. The manager must create an environment in which all members may contribute to the limits of their ability.
3. The manager must encourage full participation on important matters, continually broadening subordinate self-direction and control.

The participants were asked to indicate: (1) to what degree each of these approaches is employed on the construction site, and (2) which approach do they consider most appropriate for the construction site.

Table 6-2 presents the summary of the responses. It shows that the traditional approach is the most commonly used. The human relations approach comes in next, while the human resources approach is rarely used on the construction site. Ninety-two percent of the experts rated the approaches in the above order.

On the second question there were significant differences among the panelists; 59% indicated the human relations approach to be the most appropriate, 19% indicated the traditional approach, and 11% considered the human resources approach to be the preferred one. Another 11% did not select any single approach, but recommended the use of a combination of two approaches.

While the panel opined that the traditional approach is currently the most commonly used on construction sites, and a majority of the partici-

TABLE 6-2 Managerial Approaches to Motivation—the Commonly Used and the Preferred

APPROACH	DEGREE OF USAGE (Median[a])	PANEL PREFERENCE (%)
Traditional	4	19
Human relations	3	59
Human resources	2	11
Combination of two approaches	—	11

[a]Scoring: Not at all = 1; To a very great degree = 5.

pants believed that the human relations approach is more appropriate, the panel agreed that in some situations management would have to progress even further and adopt a key feature of the human resources approach, namely, employee participation. There was a consensus of opinion among the panelists that for the introduction of financial incentive programs management would benefit from involving the workers in the design of the programs.

This suggested change in leadership style is in agreement with the popular contingency model of leadership.[15] This model argues that leadership style should be varied according to the situation. Jenkins and Lawler report several studies that provided clear evidence that participation by lower-level employees in the design of pay programs can improve the effectiveness of the programs.[16]

Since there is no room in the prevailing traditional management approach for employee participation and discussions about the productivity improvement programs (e.g., pay programs), one could expect great difficulties in implementing the recommendation to involve the workers in the design of the programs. Yet, the unanimous agreement among the experts on the desirability of employees' participation coupled with the reported success of such involvement are evidence of a new trend. It is reasonable to postulate, that following the example of other industries, construction will move toward more participation decision making style of leadership. It must be stressed that each company must examine the extent and the areas in which employee participation is desirable, and must tailor the involvement program to the needs of the company and the individuals therein.

CONCLUSIONS

The study concludes that the near absence of pay incentive programs in the U.S. construction industry can be attributed to: (1) tradition and conservatism of the industry; (2) the nature of the work; and (3) union opposition. Another obstacle alleged by panel members was that construction management was not sophisticated enough to administer pay incentive programs. The panel opined, however, that activation of incentive programs would improve the quality of management.

The study of the attitudes of the parties toward the introduction of pay programs suggests paying attention to: (1) The work factor due to which the parties support or oppose the introduction of pay programs. (2) The way in which the magnitude of the support or opposition compares between either different work factors for the same party or between the same factors for different parties.

As expected, the panel confirmed significant differences between the attitudes of the various parties: the contractors and the owners with a positive attitude, the employees somewhat supportive, and the union opposed. It is interesting to note that the contractors and the owners would not be swayed to oppose the programs by any work aspect. The discrepancy between the attitude of the employees and the union officials is also worth noting.

The findings have important implications. As was shown earlier the union attitude determines to a great extent if programs will be introduced or not. In order to improve the union's attitude it is important to fully understand the work aspects that induce the union to be most opposed to the programs. These work factors were identified in this study to be unemployment, rate cutting, safety, and peer relations.

The somewhat supportive attitude of the employees implies that it might be easier to introduce FIP in a nonunion environment. This conclusion is further supported by the finding that the attitude of an open shop contractor would be more positive than the attitude of a union shop contractor.

The most common remedies offered to neutralize the opposition of the parties were to publicize successful programs employed elsewhere and to embark on a variety of research projects. Specific suggestions referred to either the financial incentive programs proper or to the existing control systems.

Opinions were also conveyed that construction management would benefit from a general move toward a more participative decision making style of leadership. For the introduction of incentive programs it would have to progress even further and involve the workers in the design of the programs.

NOTES

1. John W. Kendrick, *Understanding Productivity* (Baltimore: The Johns Hopkins University Press, 1977).

2. Advisory Service for the Building Industry, *The Principles of Incentives for the Construction Industry* (London: 1969).

3. R.E. Miles et al., "Leadership Attitudes Among Public Health Officials," *American Journal of Public Health*, Vol. 56, 1966, pp. 1990-2005.

4. "Payment by Results in the Building and Civil Engineering Industry in the United Kingdom," *International Labor Review* 58, (1948): 637-43.

5. A. Entwistle and W.J. Reiners, *Incentives in the Building Industry*, National Building Studies, Special Report No. 28, H.M. Stationary Office, (London: 1958).

6. *Incentive Schemes for Small Builders*, Great Britain Department of the Environment, H.M. Stationary Office, (London: 1974).

7. "Payment by Results."

8. H.A. Linstone and M. Turoff, eds., *The Delphi Method* (Reading, Mass.: Addison-Wesley, 1975).

9. Miles et al., "Leadership Attitudes."

10. Alexander Laufer, "Assessment of Financial Incentive Programs for the Construction Labor Force: A Delphi Analysis" Ph.D. diss., The University of Texas at Austin, 1980.

11. N.C. Dalkey, et al., *Studies in the Quality of Life* (Lexington, Mass.: Lexington Books, 1972).

12. E.E. Lawler, *Pay and Organizational Effectiveness: A Psychological View* (New York: McGraw-Hill, 1971).

13. Alexander Laufer and B.E. Graham-Moore, "Attitudes Toward Productivity Pay Programs," *Journal of the Construction Division*, American Society of Civil Engineers, 1982, 109 (C04).

14. R. Marriott, *Incentive Payment Systems* (London: Staples Press, 1961).

15. F.E. Fielder, *A Theory of Leadership Effectiveness* (New York: McGraw-Hill, 1967).

16. G. Douglas Jenkins, Jr. and E.E. Lawler, "Impact of Employee Participation in Pay Plan Development," in *Organizational Behavior and Human Performance*, vol. 28, 1981, pp. 111-128.

7

Is PG Applicable to Service Sector Firms?

by Warren C. Hauck and Timothy L. Ross

We believe that the answer to the question posed by the title of this chapter is definitely yes. Quite frankly, most of the variables outlined in Chapter 1 for manufacturers are equally applicable for service firms. And, contrary to some individuals' perceptions, there are fewer measurement problems in many service sector firms when compared with some manufacturing organizations. Actual applications are more limited, however, because of the lack of interest in productivity improvement and the lack of awareness of the various systems. In this chapter, we briefly discuss the type of service industries and then review the different PG formulas as they apply. We finalize the chapter by discussing some measurement approaches that have been utilized by various service sector firms.

SERVICE SECTOR CLASSIFICATIONS

The activities commonly described as services cover a far-ranging group of organizations that share some common characteristics: output that cannot be stored and transactions that usually require direct interaction between an employee and a customer. Stanback[1] and Chase[2] remove from the services category activities that are capital-intensive and large in scale. This results in dividing the economy of the United States into the following

111

three sectors generally based on the nature of the inputs involved and the resultant outputs:

1. Primary ("Agriculture"): agriculture, fisheries, and forestry.
2. Secondary ("Industry"): manufacturing, construction, mining, transportation, communications, and public utilities.
3. Tertiary ("Service"): wholesale and retail trade; F.I.R.E. (finance, insurance, and real estate); other services (professional, personal, business, and repair); federal, state and local government.

A review of the tertiary group above suggests one common characteristic: labor-intensive operations. When this fact is blended with the previously mentioned need for direct interaction with the customer, it becomes possible to evolve a more precise service classification system that utilizes the potential for rationalization and control. Such a classification system has been devised by Chase.[3] The following four categories are based on the extent of customer contact, roughly defined as the percentage of the total transaction time that the customer must be in the system:

1. Manufacturing—literally no customer contact during the production process.
2. Quasi manufacturing—possible identifiable physical units of output.
3. Mixed service—significant exposure to direct customer contact.
4. Pure service—maximal exposure to direct customer contact; possible intangible units of service.

These categories become quite useful when managers attempt to use productivity gainsharing as a socially responsible means of achieving improvements in productivity.

PRODUCTIVITY MEASUREMENT FOR GAINSHARING

In quasi-manufacturing operations within the service sector of the economy, the availability of identifiable physical units of output and the minimal amount of customer involvement in the transaction tend to make measurement of productivity relatively easy. In fact, manufacturing firms with much indirect labor (e.g., engineering, material handlers, and maintenance) may be more difficult to measure. This is not the case in units within the mixed category such as bank tellers or hospital nurses, who have a fair amount of customer or patient contact. One reason for this is the relatively intangible dimension of quality that is included in the teller-customer or nurse-patient relationship. Frankly, the closer one moves toward pure service organizations, the more difficult becomes the task of devising "productivity measurement pure" gainsharing calculations. Pure in this sense is a performance or physical output-per-hour calculation such as Improshare, as opposed to broader measures such as multicost or even prospective forms of gainsharing such as beating budgets, which will be discussed later.

Also involved is the customer influence on the level of resources (inputs) required to provide a satisfactory service as perceived by customer (outputs) as well as the difficulty that exists in identifying and measuring these productivity components. Until recently, another factor that limited efforts to make effective use of productivity measurements in the mixed services category has been the managerial preoccupation with other aspects of the overall operation. For example, managers have been unduly concerned with marketing of services and effectiveness of services, rather than with the efficiency of service rendered. Some of the reluctance can be overcome by developing site-specific weights for the pertinent criteria which have been developed for evaluating alternative productivity gain-sharing plans.[4]

APPROPRIATE CRITERIA

Six criteria have been identified as being important to executives and to potential participants in firms considering the installation of a productivity gainsharing plan. These criteria are defined as follows:

1. *Usefulness*—the ability of the formula and/or the related calculation to assist managers and "Plan" committees to isolate problems which evolve and have an adverse impact on the unit's productivity.

2. *Understanding*—the probability that the majority of the participants can clearly grasp the nature of the formula used to measure their productivity and fully comprehend how the related "bonus pool" is computed.

3. *Fairness*—the perception of participants that the formula permits an unbiased and just distribution of the gains achieved.

4. *Soundness*—the technical accuracy and overall reliability of the formula in relating variations in the participants' contributions to changes in the productivity of their unit.

5. *Administrative ease*—a measure of the normal availability of the data required to make application of the formula used to measure productivity.

6. *Flexibility*—the ability of the calculation to be changed in order to meet rapidly changing economic conditions.[5]

At a recent conference on productivity five groups of banking and hospital executives assigned relative weights to these criteria. The weights they assigned to these criteria reflect judgments concerning their own areas of activity. In each instance, going from one criterion (such as "understand") to an operational measure of it requires careful identification of the pertinent inputs and outputs. Once this is done the criteria are less abstract, and evaluations of the various calculations are easier.

MEASUREMENT

In attempting to measure the productivity of a mixed services unit such as a hospital, it is difficult to separate productivity from "other factors because hospital output is so heterogeneous and hospital charges are a fairly unreliable guide to the relative costs needed to develop an overall output measure."[6]

One suggested approach to an output measurement system requires the use of "different weights" for different illnesses, operations, accidents, and other service requirements.[7] However, hospitals do have revenues, payroll costs, and operating expenses. Reimbursing agencies (third-party payers), which represent the major portion of hospital receipts, require detailed accounting for costs. Additionally, statistical records such as MONItrend reports provide administrators with a considerable amount of information about the hospital's operations. Therefore, despite the many problems that exist, it is quite obvious that the data required for most of the productivity gainsharing calculations are available for service sector calculations at a hospital.

In banking, there is also significant information to draw on for productivity measurement. The proper measure of banking output for use in this case can be narrowed to a choice between just two concepts: "the liquidity approach [which] is based on deposits and the transactions approach [which] is based on transactions."[8] The transactions approach is the most acceptable form by the banking industry. One PG critic suggests that "the kinds of factors that might be considered for multiple weighting among different types of activities [are] . . . number of accounts; number of checks handled; value of accounts and checks (if a factor); savings vs. checking accounts; loans, size of loans."[9] Some recent research dealing with branch bank productivity indicated that suitable weights for transactions could be developed from the relative average times required for various logical groupings of transactions. Such times need to reflect the technology in place and any other site-specific factors.[10] The most significant inputs related to these outputs are teller labor and other branch-related payroll and fringes costs.

Consideration also needs to be given to various other costs that are inputs, such as rent, depreciation, and cash variations and lossses. While the decision as to which accounts to consider for inclusion in the calculations needs to be based on a site-specific review of historical data, it is highly likely that only a few will have significant impact. In one recent study, it was suggested that the calculation include only the "teller-controllable 'Cash Variations and Losses' and 'Depreciation' (to capture the impact of electromechanical assisting and/or teller replacement equipment investments)."[11]

The above two examples (medium-sized general-care hospitals and bank branches) represent somewhat opposite extremes of the Mixed Services continuum; i.e., altruistically oriented organizations and financially dominated organizations. It is possible to develop and/or manipulate the raw data needed to evolve one or more alternative measurements suitable for each type of organization. Suitable creative analysis of other industries lying along the continuum is very possible. The nature of the useful alternative calculations is described in the following section.

ALTERNATIVE CALCULATIONS

The needs of individual service organizations as reflected in their weightings of the six criteria and the availability of data required for various calculations can differ to a considerable degree. Fortunately, the calculations that are available for use in firms considering the use of productivity gain-sharing plans cover a wide range of options. Each of the calculations normally makes use of the total net output for a relatively brief period (such as one month) and makes payments to nearly all employees (including managers and executives). A review of some of the most commonly used calculations as discussed in Chapter 3 is helpful in understanding the differences as applied to service organizations.

Improshare of Allowed Labor

Both Improshare (IMproving PROductivity through SHARing) (discussed in more detail in Chapters 2, 3, and 5) and the Allowed Labor calculations are based on the use of detailed work standards for each task required to produce a specific unit of output. These are adjusted upward to allow for related unmeasured work associated with the base labor involved in generating the output. With the requirement that detailed time standards be available for use, Improshare and Allowed Labor calculations tend to be more applicable to quasimanufacturing operations such as hospital laundries and bank check-processing operations, but other firms such as repair shops, general laundries, and schools could use such calculations quite easily with considerations for quality quite easily incorporated.

Single Ratio

The single ratio calculation is based on the simple relationship of total labor costs for the period to the total revenue. As shown in Table 7-1, it may be calculated for a typical medium-sized general-care hospital as follows:

$$\text{Single ratio} = \frac{\text{TL}}{\text{TR}} = \frac{\$295{,}000}{\$500{,}000} = 59\%$$

The major advantages of the single ratio calculation are its ease of calculation and simplicity of understanding. Most manufacturing firms would have a lower allowable percentage. As previously noted, the labor intensity of mixed-service operations permits this calculation to represent a majority of the input costs, which would obviously be broken out separately by department and/or function. Indexing could be used to adjust for the inflationary impact on revenue and wages. However, the single ratio does ignore the impact of capital and/or energy inputs on changes in output.

TABLE 7-1 General-Care Hospitals: Typical Financial Details for Use in Calculating Productivity Gainsharing Ratios

	OUTPUT		
Gross revenue	$527,000		
Loss on medicare	−25,000		
Other adjustments	−23,000		
Net revenue		$479,000	
Interest (may be excluded)		15,000	
Misc. income (may be excluded)		6,000	
Total Revenue (TR)			$500,000

	INPUTS		
Payroll		$250,000	
Fringes		45,000	
Total Labor (TL)			$295,000
Supplies and fees		$125,000	
Admin. & misc. costs		55,000	
Other Costs (OC)			$180,000

CALCULATIONS

$$\text{Single ratio} = \frac{\text{TL}}{\text{TR}} = \frac{\$295{,}000}{\$500{,}000} = 59\%$$

$$\text{Multicost ratio} = \frac{\text{TL} + \text{OC}}{\text{TR}} = \frac{\$295{,}000 + \$180{,}000}{\$500{,}000} = 95\%$$

$$\text{Value-added ratio} = \frac{\text{TL}}{\text{TR} - \text{OC}} = \frac{\$295{,}000}{\$500{,}000 - \$180{,}000} = 92\%$$

For the typical hospital being used as an example, capital expenditures frequently involve the adoption of new technology, which is often embodied in new services that are additions to, rather than replacements for, existing services.

This technology-based revenue increase is reflected in an earlier study by Berry, which indicated that hospitals with "quality-enhancing services" and "complex services" had average costs per patient day that were, respectively, 16% and 27% higher than those in a hospital with only "basic services," although the relative annual labor rates were only 12% and 21% higher.[12] Should such changes occur during the period in which the measure is intended for use, the ratio will obviously give erroneous readings of the impact of the total labor factor. Similarly, the OPEC-caused increase in energy costs, which is reflected in revenue increases, is greater than the wage increases during the same periods. Indexing of other calculation modifications could adjust for several variables, as it is done by some manufacturing firms. Numerous items could also be included or excluded from both outputs and inputs.

One problem that can occur with the single ratio is a variation in product mix over time. A common method of overcoming that problem is the use of the split ratio calculation, which is discussed in the next section. The single ratio calculation could be used in hospitals, appraisal services, consulting firms, distribution centers, government services, security services, educational institutions, and computer service firms to name a few.

Split Ratio

Essentially, the split ratio calculation is two or more single ratios, which are aligned according to the labor intensity of the services that generate the total revenue. Each of these ratios would include the directly associated labor costs and a rational allocation of the other payroll and fringes costs as shown in Table 7-1. In general, the split ratio has the same advantages and disadvantages associated with the single ratio except that it does help resolve the product mix problem. Many of the other problems that exist can be overcome by the use of a more comprehensive ratio—one that incorporates a greater percentage of the inputs required to generate the total revenue.

Two of the most common extensions of the single ratio (which can also be designed along the lines of the split ratio) are the multicost ratio and the value-added ratio. These are discussed individually in the following sections using the same typical financial data for a medium-sized general-care hospital as was used to explain the single ratio; i.e., Table 7-1. Firms that would find the split ratio more applicable include advertising agencies, architectural firms, and insurance firms.

Multicost Ratio

The inclusion of other costs (OC) essentially converts the single ratio into the multicost ratio. As shown in Table 7-1, it is calculated in the following manner:

$$\text{Multicost Ratio} = \frac{\text{TL} + \text{OC}}{\text{TR}} = \frac{\$295,000 + \$180,000}{\$500,000} = 95\%$$

While the resulting percentage will vary between service sector industries and depends on decisions concerning the specific costs to be added, the expansion normally results in a ratio that is 80% to 95% inclusive of the total revenue. This large percentage of the revenue tends to practically eliminate the problems of inflation and product mix. A problem that it creates, however, is a potential conclusion by the participants that they have no control over some of the factors included in the ratio. This calculation does have major advantages over profit sharing, such as not having to disclose profits and it still is output/input related.

If increases in various other costs cannot be fully recovered in the charges made for the services rendered, the ratio would be adversely affected. If it is not feasible to make equitable adjustments in the related calculations, then consideration can be given to making the impact less severe by subtracting the other costs (OC) from both the numerator and the denominator of the multicost ratio equation. Doing this will yield the value-added ratio, which has several advantages that are discussed in the next section.

Multicost could be applied to banks, employment agencies, executive search firms, hospitals, hotels and motels, restaurants, theaters, and many other types of establishments. It has been used in many manufacturing firms with considerable success when the orientation is toward overall organization performance.

Value-Added Ratio

As suggested above, this ratio is a simple modification of the multicost ratio. Using the data for medium-sized general-care hospital found in Table 7-1, the value-added ratio is calculated in the following manner:

$$\text{Value-added ratio:} \frac{\text{TL}}{\text{TR} - \text{OC}} = \frac{\$295,000}{\$500,000 - \$180,000} = 92\%$$

Research into the use of this ratio—which is the common basis of the Rucker Plan—indicates that it does not need to be changed for wage rate increases, changes in charges for services rendered, material cost changes, or variations in the portion of work subcontracted, all of which frequently test the single ratio. It would tend to give erroneous readings, however, following the installation of cost-effective technological improvements. Such changes would undoubtedly require a new or modified calculation for an equitable measure and/or related bonus plan.

This calculation could be used in sites where product mix is a problem, such as retail stores, job shops, theaters, and airlines, or when multi-cost is not selected for disclosure reasons.

Other Measures

In service sector companies that have a comprehensive set of standard costs, it is possible to make use of a standard labor ratio. This ratio is based on the relationship of labor costs to total standard costs (standard labor rates). It has the advantage of not needing to use total revenue in the calculation. The use of service-specific time and material measurements greatly decreases the problems of product mix and the use of performance-based data eliminates the influence of inflation.

Even broader-based measures of productivity can be developed. Such ratios deal with the return achieved on investment, assets, or stockholders' equity. The calculations required under these measures closely resemble the multicost ratio supplemented by a factor to reflect the contribution of capital assets. For example, the recently completed negotiations between Chrysler Corporation and the UAW provide that workers will get 15% of net earnings after 10% of assets. Such agreements involving profit sharing generally do represent productivity gainsharing in financial terms. They generally incorporate payment delays, lack a direct relationship to performance productivity, and have a limited ability to stimulate employee involvement.

Some organizations attempt to overcome these limitations by modifying one of the calculations discussed above in a manner that emphasizes one or more important areas of their businesses. The variety of input data and output data available within an organization can be creatively combined to develop a tailor-made hybrid calculation. This can involve the use of a series of weights to give recognition to levels of service quality, generation of incremental revenue (cross-selling of available services), or other important factors for the long-term success of the firm. Budgeted performance is sometimes used. The exact nature of the service sector industry and the site-specific, time-related weightings of the six evaluative criteria will guide the choice of the best calculation for use by individual mixed-services firms.

APPLICATION—ACTUAL AND POTENTIAL

Many calculations have been used in service organizations. Unfortunately, the calculation is often perceived by managers/owners to be more important than behaviorally oriented variables. This is seldom true, but this misperception works against PG success. From a purely pragmatic standpoint, *the objectives* of the measurement system are *more important than its form.* For example, if one wants overall performance such as return on investment or return on sales to coincide with bonuses, then one should adopt one of these measures or, preferably, multicost or value added. If no detailed measures such as multicost or something prospective like budgets or targeted performance.

In actual practice, PG has been applied in many service organizations, as the partial list given below indicates. Many service organizations also have profit sharing, which could be considered PG in a very broad sense. Some PG plans that have been brought to our attention as actual or potential applications or those that we helped install include the following:

1. *Allowed Labor:* repair shops, laundries, schools.
2. *Single Ratio:* appraisal services, consultants, distribution centers, government services, security services.
3. *Split Ratio:* advertising agencies, architects, insurance firms.
4. *Multicost Ratio:* banks, employment agencies, executive search firms, hospitals, hotels and motels, property management firms, publishing firms.
5. *Value-Added Ratio:* dental clinics, retail stores, funeral homes, nursing homes, photographic studios, restaurants, theaters.
6. *Standard Labor Ratio:* captive service operations, data processing services, dry cleaners, libraries.
7. *Profit Sharing or Return on Investment:* TV and radio broadcasting, newspaper publishing, investment companies, law firms, accounting firms, medical clinics.

In the years to come, we expect many other service firms to install gainsharing as they become familiar with its principles and with both behavioral and measurement data drawn from real-life experiences. These service firms will normally start with the simpler calculations based on the criteria of understanding, administrative ease, and so on and move to increasingly more complex calculations. In fact, much of gainsharing's future growth will be centered in service sector firms because of limited past interest and applications and increased emphasis on employee involvement in those firms.

NOTES

1. Thomas M. Stanback, Jr., *Understanding the Service Economy: Employment, Productivity, Location* (Baltimore: Johns Hopkins University Press, 1979) p. 6.

2. Richard B. Chase, "Where Does the Customer Fit in a Service Operation?," *Harvard Business Review,* November-December 1978, p. 138.

3. Ibid.

4. Victor R. Fuchs, ed., *Production and Productivity in the Service Industries,* Studies in Income and Wealth, Volume Thirty-four (New York: National Bureau of Economic Research, distributed by Columbia University Press, 1969), p. 164.

5. Paul B. Ginsburg and Lawrence A. Wilson, *Controlling Rising Hospital Costs,* (Washington, D.C.: Government Printing Office, 1979), p. 4.

6. Leon Greenberg, *A Practical Guide to Productivity Measurement* (Washington, D.C.: Bureau of National Affairs, 1973), p. 41.

7. Warren C. Hauck, "An Evaluation of Alternative Productivity Gainsharing Formulas for Use in Service Sector Industries," (Ph.D. diss., Case-Western Reserve University, 1981), pp. 63–65.

8. Carl Heyel, ed., *The Encyclopedia of Management,* 2nd ed. (New York: Van Nostrand Reinhold, 1973).

9. Ibid.

10. Ibid.

11. Stanback, *Understanding the Service Economy.*

12. Ralph E. Berry, Jr., "On Grouping Hospitals for Economic Analysis," *Inquiry* 10, December 1973, p. 10.

8

Making Productivity Programs Last

by Paul S. Goodman and James W. Dean, Jr.

In the 1970s we saw a proliferation of new forms of work organization projects designed to improve on productivity and quality of working life. In many ways the new forms of work organization projects were revolutionary because they represented fundamental changes in how work should be organized, in how organizations might be designed, and in the nature of labor-management relationships. Some examples of these new forms of work organization are discussed below.

Autonomous work groups represent one new form of work organization project. Basically, these are self-governing groups organized by process, place, or product. There is a substantial shift in authority and decision making as the group takes over such responsibilities as hiring, discipline, and allocation of production tasks. Most autonomous groups encourage job switching. Pay is based on knowledge of jobs rather than actual job performance.[1]

Matrix business teams represent a restructuring of management and the workforce. First, all management—staff and line—are organized in business teams. This means that such tasks as engineering and quality control maintenance are organized not by function but are integrated into the line organization. This is accomplished by changing the authority and communications relationships as well as the physical location of team members. The teams focus on a single product or part of the production process.

Suggestions from the floor teams are sent to the business teams for processing. In the matrix business team there is no major modification of the existing pay system.

Companywide gainsharing plans are forms that include some complementary organization changes for increasing productivity. Scanlon plans, which are well described in this volume, would be included in this group.

Labor-management problem-solving groups represent another common form of change. In this type of program, a hierarchy of linked problem-solving groups is superimposed on the existing organizational structure. The groups are generally arranged following the current organizational structure, with lower-level groups dealing with problems specific to their areas, and higher-level groups dealing with problems that cut across multiple organizational units. These groups meet regularly. Products from these groups include work simplification, flextime projects, new performance appraisal systems, etc.

Many other organizational changes, such as Quality Circles (QC), job enrichment activities, and parallel business organizations, were introduced during the seventies. They all represent fundamental changes in an organization's communication, decision-making, authority, and reward systems. They also create fundamental changes in the relationships among people within the organization.

Beyond merely enumerating work organization projects, we now turn our attention to a look at whether these programs last. That is, after some period of initial success, do these productivity programs persist or remain institutionalized? Or are they just temporary phenomena? Why do some projects decline while others do not? What factors shape whether these QWL projects have some long-term viability?

SIGNIFICANCE

The importance of understanding more about the concept of persistence or institutionalization of change should be apparent. If one is interested in bringing about long-term change in productivity, the quality of working life, and labor management relationships, then we must know more about why some change programs remain viable while others decline.

Unfortunately, there are very few well-developed frameworks for understanding this problem area.[2,3] So it is difficult to go to the organizational literature to gain insights, in some systematic way, of why change programs do or do not decline over time.

Yet there is some growing evidence that many of these new forms of work organization projects do not last.[4,5] Goodman and Dean recently examined the persistence of change in a heterogeneous sample of new forms of work organization projects. They selected organizations in which the change program had been successfully introduced and where some positive benefits had been identified. Goodman and Dean interviewed participants in this organization four to five years after the project had been implemented. They wanted to know whether the change activities had persisted. Only one-third of the change programs designed to increase productivity and quality of working life exhibited some reasonable level of persistence. The other change activities were either nonexistent or in decline.

Of course, it is difficult to ascertain any national percentages about the number of these change programs that exhibit persistence. We will never know exactly how many Quality of Work Life (QWL) or new forms of work organization projects will decline and fail. However, common sense and growing empirical findings suggest that maintaining change is a significant problem for labor leaders, managers, and practitioners of organizational change.

INSTITUTIONALIZATION

A Definition

Institutionalization is examined in terms of specific behaviors or acts. We are assuming here that the persistence of QWL-type change programs can be studied by analyzing the persistence of the specific behaviors associated with each program. For example, job switching is a set of behaviors often associated with autonomous work groups. To say that the behaviors associated with a program are practiced is to say that the program is institutionalized. An institutionalized act then, is defined as a behavior that is performed by two or more individuals, persists over time, and exists as a part of the organization.

When we say that a behavior such as job switching is "part of the organization" we mean that members of the organization know about job switching, like to do it, and consider it appropriate for all members of the organization to job-switch. Remember, institutionalized behavior does not depend on any one individual; it is an organizational phenomenon.

Persistence is another key idea in our thinking about institutionalization. Persistence in the context of planned organizational change refers to the probability that the key behaviors in an organizational change program get performed. Such behaviors may include labor-management committee meetings, making suggestions in a scanlon plan, or job switching in an autonomous work group,

In summary, the defining characteristics of institutionalization of an organizational change program are performance of the change program behaviors, persistence of these behaviors, and the incorporation of these behaviors in the daily functioning of the organization.

Degrees of Institutionalization

It should be clear from our definition of institutionalization that an act is all or nothing. An act may vary in terms of its persistence, the number of people in the organization performing the act, and the degree to which it exists as part of the organization. The problem in some of the current literature on change is the use of the words *success* and *failure*. This language clouds the crucial issue of representing and explaining degrees or levels of institutionalization. Most of the organizational cases we have reviewed cannot be described by simple labels of success or failure. Rather, we find various degrees of institutionalization.

The basic questions are, then: What do we mean by degrees of institutionalization? How do we measure these degrees?

We have identified five factors that contribute to the degrees of institutionalization.

1. *Knowledge of the behaviors.* Remember that institutionalization is analyzed by looking at the behaviors required by the change program. Here we are interested merely in how many people know about these behaviors, and how much they know. Do they know how to perform these behaviors? Do they know the purposes of the behaviors? For example, "team meetings" are a part of many QWL programs. In some cases, people know that they are supposed to have the meetings. In this type of situation, the change program is not very institutionalized. This is why knowledge of the behaviors is important.

2. *Performance.* Here we are interested in how many people perform the behaviors, and how often they perform them. This is not quite as simple as it sounds, however. First, some behaviors are supposed to occur more often than others. A labor-management committee may be expected to meet occasionally, say, about once a month, while team meetings are held weekly. We would not say that team meetings are more institutionalized than the labor-management committee just because they are more frequent. Second, some behaviors are supposed to be performed by more people than others. Most employees would be involved in team meetings, but only a few would take part if a labor-management committee. Again, we would not want to say that the team meetings were more institutionalized than the labor-management committee. The idea is not merely to count the number of persons or the frequency of the behaviors, but rather to compare numbers and frequency to the levels required by the change program. Only then can reasonable comparisons be made.

3. *Preferences for the behaviors.* Here we are interested in how much people either like or dislike performing the behavior. In well-institutionalized change programs most organizational members will like the critical program behaviors. In change programs on the decline there generally are negative feelings expressed toward the critical program behaviors.

4. *Normative consensus.* This aspect of institutionalization measures two things: (1) how aware individuals are that other people in the organization are performing the behaviors and (2) how aware people are that other people feel they should perform the behaviors. Generally, when we see other people performing a behavior, we assume that they want to perform it, even though this may not be true. Note that this measure of institutionalization is not the same as the last two we listed. While they measure how many people perform the behaviors and how much they like or prefer them, here we are interested in people's beliefs about how many others perform and feel that they should perform the behaviors. The more people believe that people both perform and feel that they should perform the behaviors associated with the program, the more the program is institutionalized.

5. *Values.* The final measure of institutionalization is the extent to which people have developed values concerning the behaviors in the change program. Values are general ideas about how people ought to behave. For example, many change programs include behaviors consistent with the values of freedom and responsibility, as in autonomous work groups. In scanlon plans we expect to see the emergence of values of cooperation. The more people have developed these values, and the more aware they are that others have developed these values, the greater the degree of institutionalization for the change program.

The five aspects above represent measures of the degree of institutionalization. But how do we combine them to get an overall measure? The answer is relatively simple, because the five aspects of institutionalization generally occur in the order in which we presented them. First, people develop beliefs about the behaviors (1), and then they begin to perform them (2). People start to develop feelings about the behaviors (3), and others come to be aware of these feelings (4). Finally, values start to evolve concerning the behaviors (5). The further this sequence has progressed, the more the program has become institutionalized. Thus, in one program, people may know about the behaviors and perform them, but none of the other aspects may be present. In another program, the behaviors may be known, performed, liked, and supported by norms and values. The latter program is obviously more institutionalized.

Summary

A change program designed to increase productivity and quality of working life is institutionalized when the behaviors required by it are performed by two or more persons over a period of time, and persist over time. We have argued that institutionalization is not an all-or-nothing question, but a matter of degree, and we have identified five aspects of institutionalization in order to measure the degree to which it has occurred. A program is institutionalized to the extent that it has progressed from the levels of knowledge and performance to preferences, norms and values.

FACTORS THAT AFFECT INSTITUTIONALIZATION

General Framework

Now that we have a way to represent the degree of institutionalization, we can try to explain how and why it happens. Why are some QWL programs more institutionalized than others? Our opinion is that there are five processes that affect the degree of institutionalization. These processes are important in explaining why some programs decline, while others grow and persist over time. The processes are:

Training. This is a broad category, which includes the training of employees at the start of the program, training of new employees as they are hired or transfer in, and the retraining of employees at later times about features of the change program.

Commitment. This refers to how motivated people are to perform behaviors in a QWL program. High-commitment individuals invest a lot of themselves into new work behaviors, and they will resist attempts to change these behaviors. Commitment toward a new form of work behavior is enhanced when people voluntarily select that behavior in some public context.

Reward Allocation. This refers to what rewards are distributed in the program, who gives them and who gets them, and when they are distributed.

Diffusion. This refers to the extension of the behavior into new areas, to new work groups and individuals. If the behaviors are introduced in work group A, and we eventually see them being transferred to work group B, diffusion has occurred.

Feedback and Correction. These refer to the processes by which the organization can assess the degree of institutionalization, feed back information, and take corrective action. Many organizations we have observed have no way of telling how well their programs are doing. Therefore, there is no way they can take corrective actions.

We believe that these five processes are the major factors in predicting the degree of institutionalization a program will attain. There are, however, other important factors that affect these five processes. They are the structure of the change program and organizational characteristics. Structure of the change program means such things as the goals of the change, how general it is, the critical roles associated with the change (consultant, facilitator), etc. Organizational characteristics are arrangements existing in the organization prior to the change program. It is the canvas on which the program is painted. Organizational characteristics include such things as workforce skill level, labor-management relations, and existing values and norms. It should be emphasized that these factors are important only insofar as they affect the five processes listed above.

EMPIRICAL FINDINGS

This section is concerned with findings of the authors, as well as others, about the processes and other organizational factors related to institutionalization. We will consider findings about processes, the structure of the change, and organizational characteristics, to see if studies bear out what we have argued in the previous section. The main results came from a recent study by Goodman and Dean,[6] as described earlier in this paper, but the findings of other authors have been included where they are appropriate.

FIVE PROCESSES

Training

The first process to be discussed is training. Training is providing information to organizational members about the new work behaviors. There are three major situations in which training is important: training as the program is started, retraining after the program has been in place for a while, and training of new members of the organization. Most organizations do an extensive amount of initial training but are less consistent in retraining and in the training of new members.

Golembiewski and Carrigan report that retraining can lead to persistence.[7] In a program designed to change the practices of high-level managers in the sales division of a manufacturing firm, they found that a retraining exercise several months after the program was instituted strengthened the persistence of the program. Similarly, Ivancevich compared Management by Objectives programs in two large manufacturing firms.[8] One firm had a retraining exercise, while the other had none. After three years, the program in the former plant was more institutionalized. Goodman in a study of a change project in an underground coal mine, reports that a decrease in frequency of training after first year of the project contributed to its decline.[9] Organizations have also been found to differ in their attention to the training of new members, once the program is in place. Goodman and Dean[10] found that programs in which attention was paid to this type of training were likely to be more institutionalized.

Commitment

Commitment refers to how motivated people are to perform a behavior and to resist changing that behavior. Therefore, a high degree of commitment should increase the chances that behaviors in a QWL program would continue, or be institutionalized. Commitment toward a behavior is increased when people voluntarily select that behavior in some public context. A recent study by the present authors has demonstrated the importance of commitment for institutionalization.[11] For example, an autonomous work-group program seemed to grow and develop when personal choices were carried out freely. Later in the program, when the organization required others to participate in the program, it began to decline. The same study also found that programs with more frequent commitment opportunities were more institutionalized than those with limited commitment on institutionalization. For example, Ivancevich attributes the failure of a Management by Objectives program to a lack of commitment by top management.[12] Walton, on the other hand, notes high levels of commitment in several successful programs of work innovation.[13] Other studies report that consistent levels of commitment throughout the organization are necessary for persistence of a change program designed to increase productivity and quality of working life.[14]

Kiesler and his associates have performed research on commitment that is important for understanding institutionalization.[15] Their research concerns the effect on commitment of an attack on someone's beliefs. If the person is weakly committed, the attack will make him or her still weaker. But if the person is strongly committed, the threat will make him or her even stronger. These findings relate to institutionalization in the following way: One of the problems in institutionalizing a change program is turnover. New employees have not been convinced that the program is worthwhile, and so may be seen as an attack on the beliefs of the "old" employees. If this turnover occurs early in the program, while commitment is still weak, it will further weaken the program. However, if new members can be kept to a minimum until later in the program, when commitment is stronger, it may actually strengthen the program.

Reward Allocation

This is the process by which rewards are distributed to employees in connection with the change program. Three aspects of the reward allocation process are important in understanding institutionalization: (1) the types of rewards that are available, (2) the links between behaviors and rewards, and (3) problems of inequity in the distribution of the rewards.

Psychologists place rewards that are available from work in two categories: extrinsic and intrinsic. Extrinsic rewards are those, such as pay and promotion, that are given by someone else. Intrinsic rewards are those, such as feelings of responsibility and accomplishment, that come from within the individual. Many organizational change programs have been based on the assumption that intrinsic rewards are sufficient for institutionalization. However, Goodman and Walton have questioned this assumption.[16,17] In the recent study by the present authors, programs that combine both extrinsic and intrinsic rewards have attained the highest degree of institutionalization, while programs with intrinsic rewards alone have been less institutionalized.

The second issue in reward allocation concerns the link between the behaviors required by the change program and the rewards. It is important that the rewards be linked to the actual performance of the behaviors, as opposed to mere participation in the program. We have found that there is a higher degree of institutionalization in programs where the link between performance and rewards is strong. This is consistent with statements by Vroom and Lawler concerning reward allocation.[18,19]

A final issue concerning reward allocation is the potential for problems of inequity. Problems of inequity occur when an employee feels he is not being fairly compensated for the work he is doing. Results of studies have shown that new programs often become complicated by problems of inequity. For example, Locke, Sirota, and Wolfson report on a job-enrichment program in a government agency that did not become institutionalized.[20] The major reason for this was that the workers were not compensated financially for the new skills they had learned. It is important to note that they had never been promised more money, but the fact that they were accomplishing more for the same pay was perceived as inequitable. Goodman reports similar problems to develop autonomous work groups in a coal mine.[21] Part of the program involved job switching, whereby each new member would eventually learn all the jobs in the crew. The problem was that the entire crew was to be paid at the same (higher) rate, which originally was paid only to certain crew members. Since it had taken years for some of the men to attain this rate, they felt it inequitable that the other crew members should come upon it so easily. This contributed to the decline of the change program.

Diffusion

Diffusion refers to the spread of the change program from one part of an organization to another. Diffusion is significant because the more the change program becomes diffused, the stronger the institutionalization. As long as the program is restricted to one part of the organization, people may not feel compelled to take it seriously or they may object to it. But as diffusion starts to occur, people in other parts of the organization will begin to consider whether they should participate. As the program spreads, there also are chances for counterattacks on its validity.

The importance of diffusion for institutionalization has been noted by Goodman in the coal mine study mentioned above.[22] In this case, when the intervention failed to diffuse beyond the original target group, it was perceived as inappropriate and failed to become institutionalized. Similar findings have been reported in a study of work teams in several plants of a large manufacturing company. When the innovations continued to be limited to a few parts of the organization, they were seen as inappropriate to the company as a whole and failed to become institutionalized. However, the researchers in this study caution against diffusion that is too rapid, as widespread understanding, acceptance, and resources are necessary to support such an effort. Without these prerequisites, the program will collapse under its own weight. In general then, a medium course must be found between no diffusion and diffusion that is too ambitious for the resources supporting it.

Feedback and Correction

Sensing and correction are the processes by which the organization finds out how well the program is doing and takes steps to correct problems that have emerged. One of the common findings in our study was that what was actually occurring in the programs was often different from what was intended.[23] That is, the organizations seldom had any formal way of detecting whether the intended change was in place. Only in the most institutionalized programs in our study did mechanisms exist for feedback and correction. Walton, who has undertaken a number of case studies of organizational change, says that the lack of feedback and correction mechanisms is a major cause of the failure to institutionalize.[24] In another study, feedback mechanisms were in place, so that information about the progress of the program was available.[25,26] However, no one ever did anything about the problems that were detected. Perhaps the information was not available to those who had the power to do something. Or perhaps the information was available to them, and there were other reasons for their inaction. In any case, both sensing and correction mechanisms are important in attaining a high degree of institutionalization.

STRUCTURE OF THE CHANGE

Now that we have discussed the findings about the processes, we can discuss some of the factors that affect the processes. First, we will discuss the structure of the change, which refers to the unique aspects of the change program. Specifically, we will talk about the goals of the programs, the formal mechanisms associated with the programs, the level of intervention in the programs, how consultants were used, and sponsorship for the programs.

Goals

One way to characterize goals is by whether they are specific and limited or general and diffuse. In our study,[27] we found that programs designed to improve productivity or quality of working life with specific goals became more institutionalized than those with diffuse goals.

Another way to characterize goals is by whether they are common or complementary. Common goals were ones that are desired by both parties to the change (for example, improving safety). Complementary goals aim to give each party something it wants, but the parties want different things (for example, productivity for management and bonuses for employees). Goodman indicates that common goals can contribute better to institutionalization.[28]

Formal Mechanisms

Most change programs have some new organizational form and procedures associated with them. These include the hierarchy of groups found in the parallel organization, the self-governing decisions made by autonomous work groups, etc. Here we are interested in how formal these arrangements are. For example, are meetings scheduled in advance? Are procedures written down? In general, we have found that programs with more formal mechanisms and procedures attain higher levels of institutionalization.

Level of Intervention

Here we are interested in whether the QWL program was introduced in a part of the organization, or in the whole organization. In our study, programs that were introduced throughout the whole organizational unit became more institutionalized than programs limited to a part of the organization. One of the problems with smaller-scale intervention is that people from other parts of the organization sometimes attempt to sabotage the program. This was true in four of the organizations that we studied, none of whose programs were very institutionalized.[29]

Consultants

Most organizations that undertake a change program employ a consultant to help them. This is true of the organizations we recently studied. Some organizations use consultants for considerably longer periods of time than others. We found that firms that rely on consultants for a long time are less able to develop their own capacity for managing the program. Consequently, after the consultant leaves, they are less able to institutionalize the program. The greater the dependence on the consultant, the less successful the program.

Sponsorship

Another factor that appears to affect the degree of institutionalization is the presence of a sponsor. The sponsor is an organizational member in a position of power who initiates the program, makes sure that resources are devoted to it, and defends it against attacks from others in the organization. If the sponsor leaves the organization, usually no one steps in to perform these necessary functions, and processes such as commitment and reward allocation are hampered, thus making it harder for institutionalization to occur. In our study, the initial sponsor was still present in organizations that had more institutionalized programs, but programs whose sponsors had left were low in institutionalization.

The withdrawal of sponsorship can arise from common organizational practices rather than be due to the change project. For example, Crockett reports a major organizational intervention in the State Department, in which substantial changes were observed to persist for years.[30] However, when the initiator of the project, a political appointee, left office, the organization reverted to its traditional form. The new administrator was not sympathetic to the values and the structure of the change program. As support and legitimacy of the program decreased, the degree of institutionalization declined. Similar effects are reported by Walton (the sponsors of the famous Topeka Experiment leaving the organization)[31] and by Levine (an innovative college president leaving after instituting a new structure for the school).[32] In some cases, the sponsor left temporarily;[33] in other cases, the sponsors focused attention on other organizational matters.[34] In all cases, however, the persistence of the new structures declines.

ORGANIZATIONAL CHARACTERISTICS

Organizational characteristics are those aspects of the organization that exist prior to the change program and have an effect on the degree of institutionalization a program can attain. These characteristics are important to the extent that they affect the processes we have discussed (commitment, diffusion, etc.).

Congruence with Organizational Values and Structure

Whatever the nature of the change program, one important factor for institutionalization is the extent of congruence or incongruence between the change program and existing organizational properties. In general, the more congruence, the greater will be the likelihood of institutionalization. Various organizational characteristics may be important in understanding congruence. In the cases studied by the present authors, congruence between the change program and management philosophy led to higher degrees of institutionalization.

Several other authors have come to similar conclusions about congruence and institutionalization. Fadem suggests that the greater the incongruence between the change program and corporate policies, the less likely that the project will be institutionalized.[35] Seashore and Bowers explain the level of institutionalization in terms of the congruence between the organizational change and the values and motives of the individual participant.[36] They found that a higher level of institutionalization resulted when the changes were more congruent with the values and motives of the employees. Mohrman et al. studied organizational change in a school system.[37] They found that change programs were more likely to become institutionalized when the intervention structure was congruent with the existing authority system. Walton has shown that in some change programs there is a gap between the behaviors required by the change and the skills possessed by the employees. The greater the gap (or the more incongruence), the lower will be the expected degree of institutionalization.

Levine describes a set of innovations attempted at a state university.[39] Some of the innovations were more congruent with organizational norms and values than others. Over time, those innovations that were congruent were more likely to persist than those that were incongruent. Similar conclusions were drawn by Warwick and Crockett concerning a major organizational change undertaken in the State Department.[40,41] The new structure favored the taking of initiative by lower-level officials, which was incongruent with both the reward system and received wisdom about how to be successful at the State Department. Not surprisingly, the change did not last. Finally, Miller shows that a change program must be congruent with cultural norms and values, as well as with those peculiar to the organization.[42] An organizational innovation in several weaving mills in India was hampered because it did not provide for the workers' need for recognition by superiors, which is strong in the Indian culture.

In summary, we have shown that programs can decline as a result of incongruence with existing organizational or cultural norms and values, the organizational authority system, or individual skills and motives. Of course, if these are already in conflict with one another, it will be difficult for programs to be congruent with all of them.

Stability of the Environment

From the evidence reported so far, it should be clear that institutionalizing a change program in an organization is a difficult task, even in the best of situations. Adding instability to the situation only makes things worse. In our study, there were only two cases of instability in the environment.[43] In these cases there was a major decline in demand for the organization's products, which led to curtailments in the workforce. This in turn changed the composition of many of the groups that were an integral part of the change program. These groups became less effective, which lowered the degree of institutionalization. Similar results were in another study as an economic recession led to layoffs and bumping.[44] Environment instabilities such as these represent a major obstacle to institutionalization.

Union

The union can play a major role in determining the degree of institutionalization. Many of the new forms of work organization changes run in parallel with other union-management activities related to the traditional collective-bargaining process. If there are high levels of labor-management conflict in the collective-bargaining area, we expect these to spill over to the productivity and quality of working life activities and negatively affect their viability.

Most local unions are part of larger institutional structures. In other studies there is evidence that the quality of the relationship between the local district and the international has a critical impact on the viability of any change program in a given firm.[45]

HOW DO YOU MAKE QWL PROGRAMS LAST?

The above discussion identifies a set of factors that can contribute to the persistence of productivity and other similar types of labor-management programs. It is important for the reader to remember that these factors to promote institutionalization, which are reintroduced below, are based on empirical findings, not just on the opinions of the authors.

What should we do to make QWL programs last?

1. **Selecting of Organizations.** Some organizations simply should not get involved in QWL-type change programs. A careful diagnosis is needed to be sure an organization is or is not ready. The more that labor and

management can acknowledge that some of their organizational units should not get involved, the more realistic their working relationship and the more likely that a change program, when initiated, will last. Some of the reasons for not getting involved include:

   a. *Unstable economic environments.* Organizations experiencing economic instability and high fluctuations in their labor force will be hard put to mount a successful long-run QWL effort.
   b. *Instability in leadership environment.* If there is likely to be turnover in key labor or management sponsors of the change program, it is best to delay the start of a program or abandon it.
   c. *Mistrust between employees and management or union and management.* If there are some basic problems in the relationships between employees and employers or union and management, a QWL change effort should not be introduced. QWL-type programs are not quick fixes for current labor and management ills. These problems need to be solved before QWL is considered.

2. **Plan for Institutionalization in the Beginning.** In most of the labor-management change programs we have reviewed, attention has been devoted largely to starting up a program. Little attention has been given to maintaining the program. We think that is a mistake. Mechanisms for maintaining a program need to be considered in the early planning stages. That is, the maintenance of a program needs to be designed into the front end of a program.

3. **The Fit Problems.** There needs to be a good fit between the organization's values, philosophy, and structure and the nature of the change program. The basic problem is that when the proposed change program (e.g., autonomous work groups) is in conflict with the organization's value system (high authoritarian) it simply will not last. What do we do then if we have a low-trust, high-authoritarian hierarchical system and we want to move toward a more participative system? The answer has to be in a carefully designed evolutionary change program that will occur over an extended time period.[46]

4. **Characteristics of Changes.** While there is no one program for all organizations, we should look for the following characteristics to insure a long-run effort.

   a. *Specific statement on goals, written out and legitimated by labor and management.*
   b. *Specific procedures to implement the labor and management program activities.* Running QWL activities is a complex process. Failure to clarify these processes can lead to trouble. Where feasible we think there should be some formalization of issues such as who should be in the labor management committee, when it should meet, how members should rotate, what are the boundaries of the commit-

tee's work. Formalization increases long-run viability of the change program.

   c. *Total system intervention.* Change programs that can be introduced into the total organizational unit, rather than in a part, will last longer, but only if sufficient organizational resources are allocated to them.

5. **Training over Time.** Most labor-management programs have advocated training to start up a program. We advocate periodic retraining over time to reaffirm the QWL principles to maintain the program. Special training programs for new organizational members is necessary to insure long-run viability.

6. **Commitment.** High commitment will facilitate the persistence of most labor-management change programs. High commitment comes from (1) voluntary participation in QWL activities and (2) opportunities for recommitment over time. QWL programs that offer opportunities for recommitment exhibit higher levels of persistence.

7. **Effective Reward Systems.** The design of organizational reward systems can substantially determine the longevity of a QWL program. The reward system should:

   a. *Include both extrinsic (e.g., pay) and intrinsic (e.g., more autonomy) rewards.*

   b. *Link rewards to specific behaviors required by the QWL program (e.g., assuming greater decision-making responsibilities).*

   c. *Introduce a mechanism to revise reward system.* It is unlikely rewards will maintain their attractiveness over time. A successful program will need some procedure, legitimated by labor and management, to revise rewards over time.

   d. *Minimize problems of inequity over compensation issues.* QWL programs that have not included extrinsic and intrinsic rewards, that have not tied rewards and performance together, that have not revised reward systems over time and experienced inequity, have not survived.

8. **Diffusion.** As the QWL program is introduced in one unit (e.g., a plant) it must be quickly spread to other adjacent organizational units. QWL programs in isolation will have trouble in persisting.

9. **Feedback and Correction.** One major characteristic of many QWL failures we have studied is that there were no mechanisms by which the organization could learn whether QWL activities were actually functioning or how well they were functioning. The designers of the QWL effort expected that certain behaviors such as labor-management meetings, job switching, suggesting making, and follow-up, were being performed. But they were either not being performed or not being performed well. A direct and accurate feedback mechanism which measures the perfor-

mance of QWL activities is necessary if the change program is to adjust, grow, and remain viable over time.

CONCLUSION

The best way to conclude this discussion is to repeat the basic conclusions of this paper. First, many productivity and quality of working life programs, although initially successful, do not persist over time. Second, we now know some of the critical processes—socialization, commitment, reward allocation, diffusion, feedback—that affect the long-run viability or the failure of these programs. Lastly, a set of action plans were presented to insure the long-run viability of these programs.

NOTES

1. Paul S. Goodman, *Assessing Organizational Change: The Rushton Quality of Work Experiment* (New York: Wiley-Interscience, 1979).

2. Paul S. Goodman and J.W. Dean, Jr., "The Process of Institutionalization" (paper prepared for conference on organizational change, Carnegie-Mellon University, May 1981). To be published in a forthcoming volume on organizational change, Paul S. Goodman, ed.

3. R.E. Walton, "Establishing and Maintaining High Commitment Work Systems," in *The Organizational Life Cycle,* ed. J.R. Kimberly and R.H. Miles (San Francisco: Jossey-Bass, 1980).

4. Phillip H. Mirvis and D.N. Berg, eds., *Failures in Organization Development and Change* (New York: Wiley-Interscience, 1977).

5. Goodman and Dean, "The Process of Institutionalization."

6. Ibid.

7. Robert I. Golembiewski and S.B. Carrigan, "The Persistence of Laboratory-Induced Changes in Organizational Styles." *Administrative Science Quarterly,* 15(1970): 330–40.

8. John M. Ivancevich, "Changes in Performance in a Management by Objectives Program," *Administrative Science Quarterly,* 19(1974): 563–74.

9. Goodman, *Assessing Organizational Change.*

10. Goodman and Dean, "The Process of Institutionalization."

11. Ibid.

12. John M. Ivancevich, "A Longitudinal Assessment of Management by Objectives," *Administrative Science Quarterly,* 17(1972): 126–38.

13. Walton, "Establishing High Commitment Work Systems."

14. Goodman, *Assessing Organizational Change.*

15. C.A. Kiesler, *The Psychology of Commitment: Experiments Linking Behavior to Belief* (New York: Academic Press, 1971).

16. Goodman, *Assessing Organizational Change.*

17. Walton, "Establishing High Commitment Work Systems."

18. Victor H. Vroom, *Work and Motivation* (New York: Wiley, 1964).

19. Edward E. Lawler, *Pay and Organizational Effectiveness* (New York: McGraw-Hill, 1971).

20. Edwin A. Locke, D. Sirota, and A.D. Wolfson, "An Experimental Case Study of the Successes and Failures of Job Enrichment in a Government Agency," *Journal of Applied Psychology,* 61(1976): 701–11.

21. Goodman, *Assessing Organizational Change.*

22. Ibid.

23. Goodman and Dean, "The Process of Institutionalization."

24. Walton, "Establishing High Commitment Work Systems."

25. Paul S. Goodman, personal correspondence.

26. R.E. Walton, "Teaching an Old Dog Food New Tricks," *The Wharton Magazine,* Winter 1979, pp. 38–47.

27. Goodman and Dean, "The Process of Institutionalization."

28. Goodman, *Assessing Organizational Change.*

29. Goodman and Dean, "The Process of Institutionalization."

30. W. Crockett, "Introducing Change to a Government Agency," in *Failures in Organizational Development: Cases and Essays for Learning,* ed. Phillip Mirvis and D. Berg (New York: Wiley-Interscience, 1977).

31. Walton, "Teaching an Old Dog Food New Tricks."

32. A. Levine, *Why Innovation Fails* (Albany: State University of New York Press, 1980).

33. L.L. Frank and J.R. Hackman, "A Failure of Job Enrichment: The Case of the Change That Wasn't," *Journal of Applied Behavioral Science,* 11, no. 4(1975): 413–36.

34. R.E. Walton, "The Diffusion of New Work Structures: Explaining Why Success Didn't Take," *Organizational Dynamics,* Winter 1975, pp. 3–21.

35. J. Fadem, *Fitting Computer-Aided Technology to Workplace Requirements: An Example* (paper presented at the 13th Annual Meeting and

Technical Conference of the Numerical Control Society, Cincinnati, March 1976).

36. Stanley E. Seashore and D.G. Bowers, "Durability of Organizational Change," in *Organization Development: Theory, Practice, and Research,* ed. W.L. French, C.H. Bell, Jr., and R.A. Zawicki (Dallas: Business Publications, 1978).

37. S.A. Mohrman, et al., "A Survey Feedback and Problem Solving Intervention in a School District: 'We'll Take the Survey But You Can Keep the Feedback,'" in *Failures in Organizational Development: Cases and Essays for Learning,* ed. Phillip Mirvis and D. Berg (New York: Wiley-Interscience, 1977).

38. Walton, "Establishing High Commitment Work Systems."

39. Levine, *Why Innovation Fails.*

40. D.P. Warwick, *A Theory of Public Bureaucracy* (Cambridge, Mass.: Harvard University Press, 1975).

41. Crockett, "Introducing Change."

42. E.J. Miller, "Socio-Technical Systems in Weaving, 1953–1970: A Follow-up Study," *Human Relations,* 28, no. 4(1975): 349–86.

43. Goodman and Dean, "The Process of Institutionalization."

44. Paul S. Goodman, personal correspondence.

45. Goodman, *Assessing Organizational Change.*

46. Goodman and Dean, "The Process of Institutionalization."

9

Why PG Fails in Some Firms

by Timothy L. Ross

Most experts in the field of productivity gainsharing would probably say that the success rate of PG programs is not over 65%. That does not even include firms with marginal plans, which are common. Frankly, no one really knows the failure rate, since most of the plans have been installed by consultants who are frequently unwilling to share their client's experience with others.

Failure of PG is probably associated with the managerial expectation of increased productivity. Disenchantment may set in if this doesn't occur. Likewise, if employees expect significant bonuses without major behavioral changes regarding productivity increases, they are likely to become discouraged if this does not occur.

We could state very simply that firms not developing the variables as outlined in Chapter 1 to a significant degree would probably be in an excellent position for having their plans fail and not be off the mark by far. For firms that have their plans fail in high probability exhibit the following characteristics to an extensive degree.

A. Organization Variables
   1. Low trust or confidence in management, low accountability and low levels of participation.
   2. Poor communications between/with departments and primarily from the top down.

    3. Inability to relate to the system.
    4. Low control over sales and unstable employment.
    5. Low levels of identity with organization, its past, present, and future opportunities and problems.
    6. Inequitable wages when compared with other employees and area firms.
B. Social/Cultural/Institutional
    1. Poor industrial relations and confidence.
    2. Low level needs for democratic principles.
C. Financial/Information/Competition
    1. Poor internal information system.
    2. Lack of reliability in the financial system.
    3. Low levels of financial understanding or ability to relate to the system.
    4. Lack of knowledge of or dedication to beat competition.
    5. Unstable conditions in output or input markets.
    6. Severe competitive conditions.
    7. Severe governmental constraints.

Although a few items from the model in Chapter 1 were omitted as being marginally applicable, the vast majority are applicable to PG failures. But if one analyzes them carefully, one should not be surprised to note that they are the variables commonly cited as important to the success of any organization. That is, if the company is unsuccessful, in all likelihood its gainsharing plan is doomed to failure unless drastic actions are taken. Thus, to be successful as a gainsharing company, a need to change or to be better than others must exist. Without this need to change or to be better than others, neither the employees nor management are likely to make the changes necessary on a continuing basis and the system will likely fail.

SOME EVIDENCE FROM THE LITERATURE

Several studies have attempted to explore correlates of gainsharing success. For example, Ruh, Wallace, and Frost contrasted managerial attitudes in 10 firms with active gainsharing systems with those in 8 firms that had implemented and abandoned their plans, in order to assess the differences in managerial attitudes. Their general findings were as follows:

1. Managers in firms that abandoned their plans perceived the rank-and-file employees to demonstrate significantly less judgment, creativity, responsibility, dependability, pride in performance, initiative, self-confidence, and willingness to change as compared with the perceptions of managers in firms with continuing PG plans.

2. Managers in abandoned plan firms have less favorable attitudes toward participative decision making than continuing firms' managers. The same results were found regarding the perceived impact of participation on morale and performance.[1]

Of the abandoned plan firms, the expectations of managers regarding success were negative either before or after installation. Nevertheless, the firms obviously did not sink into bankruptcy or experience other dire consequences as a result of gainsharing failure.

Although generally congruent with our predictions, the study did not validate any cause/effect variables in that the failure of the plans may have been caused by the poor attitudes or have been the effect of them. Obviously, such pregainsharing attitudes as these could spell failure. But variables outlined above could also have actually caused the abandonment of the plans and, as is often the case, differentiating and isolating the cause/effect variables is difficult.

White found a number of corroborative pieces of evidence in his study of 23 gainsharing firms, 12 of which had abandoned the plan at the time of the study.[2] All were manufacturing firms. Some of his major findings written in a negative context follow.

1. High levels of failure are associated with low levels of employee participation. That is, if participation is perceived by employees to be low, the plan is likely to be marginally effective and perhaps doomed to failure.

2. Larger size does not seem to be a major factor for failure. (Obviously one must be committed to communications and "line-of-sight" becomes important for employees to relate to the system in larger firms because of complexities but the potential benefits also increase.)

3. Low levels of managerial attitudes toward participative management are strongly associated with failure or marginal success. This variable should be useful in predicting gainsharing success if the system is participation-oriented.

4. The longer the plan is in existence, the lower the chance of abandonment. High expectations of immediate change will likely meet with disappointments. (Some long-standing firms do of course eventually abandon the plan because of economic downturns, managerial changes at the top and so on.)

5. When installing a plan, favorable expectations if realistic are important. Consequently, organizations with poor employee attitudes should not be selected for installation. Likewise, getting the proper people involved at the beginning is important.

6. If a high-level executive does not take a leading role, the plan's failure probably increases.

7. Technology does not seem to be positively or negatively related to failure.

Numerous other researchers have hypothesized problem areas and possible failure from a series of cases or "conjectures" over the years. Although these are of course not definitive, they do provide valuable insights into the forces that may occur in an actual situation and consequently supply caveats for those interested in possible problems on an a priori basis. They are not listed in order of importance but generally expand on the studies discussed above.

1. Poor calculation[3,4,5,6]
2. Lack of bonuses or opportunities for them[7,8]
3. Poor union/management cooperation and leadership[9,10,11,12,13]
4. Lack of supervisors' commitment[14,15,16,17]
5. Management defensiveness[18,19,20]
6. Lack of management's commitment of time, money, or enthusiasm[21,22,23,24,25]
7. Little need to change or be different[26,27]
8. Poor communications/information[28,29,30]
9. Lack of support for continuance from the top of the organization[31]

The evidence seems to substantiate many of our propositions. If future researchers and businessmen would utilize the model, we feel that most of the variables included would provide extremely useful information to assist in predicting both success and failure. A successful gainsharing system does not occur by chance but rather is carefully developed as well as nurtured over the years. It can survive managerial succession if support from the top is high.

THREE NEW STUDIES

In the following sections three analyses made by Ross are examined. The first is a general study of accountants and supervisors. The second is a record of an actual failure with the employees voting for abandoning the plan after a year's trial period. The third situation is a comparison between a successful plan in a very trying situation and one of limited success. The data and identity of all are disguised for purposes of anonymity.

Accountants and Supervisors Contrasted

In an attempt to partially validate primarily the financial aspects of our model, a group of 22 accountants (mostly controllers) and supervisors at existing gainsharing firms were requested to rank a set of 22 variables from very important (1) to very unimportant (5) to gainsharing success. These variables ranged from bonus earning opportunities (number 1) to departmental goal setting (number 22). A day was then spent discussing the implications of the findings. The overall findings are outlined on Table 9-1.

TABLE 9-1 Variables Important to Gainsharing Success/Failure

Check the appropriate line	Accountants	Supervisors	1 Very important	2 Important	3 Undecided	4 Unimportant	5 Very unimportant
	MEANS						
1. Bonus earning opportunities	1.6	1.4	_____	_____	_____	_____	_____
2. Understanding of the calculation	1.9	2.2	_____	_____	_____	_____	_____
3. Accuracy of standards	2.6	1.4	_____	_____	_____	_____	_____
4. Knowledge of competition	2.8	1.8	_____	_____	_____	_____	_____
5. Stability of selling market	2.3	1.6	_____	_____	_____	_____	_____
6. Trust in accounting staff	1.7	1.4	_____	_____	_____	_____	_____
7. Market growth potential	2.4	1.6	_____	_____	_____	_____	_____
8. Simplicity of calculation	2.7	1.8	_____	_____	_____	_____	_____
9. Type of work force	2.4	2.0	_____	_____	_____	_____	_____
10. Government constraints	3.2	2.3	_____	_____	_____	_____	_____
11. Knowledge of company's (plant's) performance	1.3	1.2	_____	_____	_____	_____	_____
12. Accuracy of production/inventory control system	2.0	1.4	_____	_____	_____	_____	_____
13. Trust in accounting system	1.3	1.2	_____	_____	_____	_____	_____
14. Stability of materials market	2.6	1.8	_____	_____	_____	_____	_____
15. Success of company (profit)	1.3	1.4	_____	_____	_____	_____	_____
16. Product pricing practices	1.9	1.6	_____	_____	_____	_____	_____
17. Frequency of new products	2.0	1.8	_____	_____	_____	_____	_____
18. Control over sales growth	2.5	1.6	_____	_____	_____	_____	_____
19. Current pay levels	2.5	1.4	_____	_____	_____	_____	_____
20. Stability of employment	1.9	1.4	_____	_____	_____	_____	_____
21. Departmental performance feedback	1.4	1.2	_____	_____	_____	_____	_____
22. Departmental goal setting	1.6	1.2	_____	_____	_____	_____	_____

Highly ranked by both groups included:

1. Bonus earning opportunities;
2. Trust in accounting staff;
3. Knowledge of company's (plant's) performance;
4. Trust in accounting system;
5. Success of company (profit);
6. Departmental performance feedback;
7. Departmental goal setting.

Obviously, any actions or programs directed in these areas should contribute significantly to success or failure if the results are validated for all groups of managers.

Regarding areas of significant differences between the two groups, five areas in particular stand out. These are:

1. Accuracy of standards (2.6 for accountants vs. 1.4 for supervisors).
2. Knowledge of competition (2.8 vs. 1.8).
3. Government constraints (3.2 vs. 2.3).
4. Control over sales growth (2.5 vs. 1.6).
5. Current pay levels (2.5 vs. 1.4).

In all cases, supervisors perceived them to be of more importance than did accountants. Each was discussed in detail including the reasons for the differences and how to close the gap. The results follow.

In most cases, standards do not affect the bonus directly. If they do, then their accuracy is very important, even as perceived by accountants. If they are just tools of performance expectations, then they are less important directly to gainsharing as perceived by the participants. Supervisors perceived accuracy of standards to be more important to success than did accountants. But everyone agreed that accurate standards are important to a successful firm for a variety of reasons. Most agreed on the undesirability of standards that are too loose. Supervisors also seemed to want to become more involved in the whole standards area, a good opportunity for more involvement. No significant ideas were offered to help get people to overcome the fear of changing standards. One idea was to disseminate the results of only the best workers. Another was to get people involved in the standard-setting process.

Regarding control over sales growth, supervisors again believed that this was more important, due mainly to inefficiencies that result when production is pushed too greatly or has strong ups and downs. This probably affects a supervisor's tasks more than the accountant's. Supervisors desire more stability. One participant compared uncontrolled growth to a form of cancer.

Supervisors also believed pay levels to be more important because of the inability to retain employees if pay is low. They have a strong need to maintain a stable and skilled work force.

Knowledge of competition was extensively discussed. Some points made included: (1) Accountants more than supervisors realize how complex this issue is. (2) This may be more important to sales than to production. (3) The area needs to be more heavily emphasized for all gainsharing firms of the future.

Although differences occurred regarding government constraints, both groups relegated this to low status.

Although the differences between the accountants and supervisors on trust of accounting staff and understanding of the calculation were not great, the participants believed that both are of about equal importance.

People can relate to broader calculations but they are frustrated by their inability to do much about them. An effort must be made to get to the lowest common denominator to increase understanding of line of sight concept. Few people fully understand the calculation, so much more effort needs to be expended in this area.

Most participants agreed that one need not have a bonus in the short run but that expectations for a future bonus are important. (Some newer gainsharing participants disagreed, since the bonus is a common goal.) Some perceived the bonus as an add-on but some did not; goal clarity is at issue here. Others viewed the participative management aspect as the most important aspect. But how far can one go without a bonus? Much disagreement existed on this point.

The question was asked, Do people really want to be involved? Movement is toward more participation even if workers resist. Many employees want more from their job than just money. But it takes much effort to get them to participate in a PG program. If they do become involved, problems can result if they don't continue their involvement.

Another inquiry area focused on whether a plan could be successful if everyone knew that a bonus would not be earned without a large layoff or other drastic measures? Much disagreement existed on this point. Most believed that it would be a mistake to sell it on this basis. The key is to get everyone to be improvement oriented from top management down. Expectations can, of course, get too high to attain.

The key question brought up by most is, What turns an employee or group on? This is the key to measuring success. To some it is money or bonus, but to others, it might be involvement or recognition. If employees relate strongly to bonuses, then they should understand why one is or is not being earned.

An extensive discussion took place regarding whether people should know who is and who is not earning or contributing to the bonus, a possibility to document with some calculations. This can be divisive but also can be quite constructive, depending on how used. Who really earns and contributes to a bonus is frequently difficult to establish because of the complexities of cause and effect.

Likewise, considerable differences were expressed regarding how much individual recognition should occur. Most agreed that the best recognition is of the type in which the entire organization is recognized. Effort should also concentrate on both low and high performers.

A Case of Failure

This is a fairly brief case of a gainsharing failure. The background is as follows:

1. A small (60 employee) manufacturing (primarily assembly operation) firm in a depressed area of a large city.

2. The highest profit in the previous five years before installation of the PG plan less than 1% of sales before corporate charges and interest. No profits for four out of the five years.

3. Predominantly minority workforce with low wages (approximately 50 cents above minimum wage requirements); low skill level.

4. Market declining; sales decreasing in absolute dollars.

5. Part of a major conglomerate.

6. "Last chance" for improving the performance of the firm.

7. Unionized but no interference from local. In fact, wage concessions obtained.

8. Weak financial information system.

9. Training and other activities severely limited by financial conditions.

A behavioral evaluation was conducted, including an employee survey. A management team effectiveness profile indicated low evaluation of fellow managers, especially the president. A survey of employee attitudes indicated the following key summarized results. The survey was on a five-point Likert type of scale with 5 being the highest mean and 1 being the lowest.

		Mean
1.	How satisfied would you say you are with your earnings?	2.36
2.	How would you rate cooperation between departments?	2.40
3.	How would you rate communications between departments?	2.20
4.	To what extent do you have confidence and trust in your supervisor?	2.90
5.	Is management willing to accept suggestions you make?	2.74
6.	Is the take-home pay here as good as similar companies in the area?	2.20
7.	Do you feel that the pay for your job is fair compared with the pay for other jobs in this plant?	2.10
8.	The feeling of satisfactory relationships with management?	2.20
9.	How much confidence and trust is there in management?	2.00
10.	How much concern is there for controlling costs?	2.60

Obviously, conditions were poor for the installation of a plan on several key variables:

1. Because of very low earnings employees would probably perceive of the plan as a substitute for equitable wages.

2. Poor communications were apparent.
3. Little trust in management existed and little reason to trust them.
4. Supervisors were poorly trained.
5. There was low concern for controlling costs.
6. Written comments indicated severe feelings of discrimination, pressure for performance, and poor equipment.

Additional problems centered on inadequate available time or money. Finally, neither employees nor managers perceived a real need to change in spite of the financial conditions. Also, they had low levels of expectations in general on eight key questions regarding such activities as costs, quality, productivity, job security, and need for involvement.

When the plan was finally presented to the employees following the completion of the work of a steering committee, a confidential vote was taken for a trial period of one year. The vote was exactly 75%, too low a commitment for good initial success. (Note: it was requested that the president not be present or many employees would definitely vote against the plan.)

This was, of course, a high-risk situation at best. However, the plant and divisional management believed that little could be lost by trying the plan even though they were cautioned against thinking it could work. Quite simply, they were told to do something—and plans had saved other firms from going under.

The results of the first and only year of operation are outlined below:

1. A major layoff in the first month of operation resulted in a one-third reduction of the workforce. Three layoffs occurred the first year.
2. Bonuses were not paid until the fourth month of operation (5.1%). This was the largest of four bonuses—3.5%, 5.0%, and 2.2% of wages, or about 1.5% for the year.
3. Volume continued to erode over the previous year; backlays continued to erode.
4. Wide fluctuations in sales and inventory made it difficult to evaluate whether direct labor productivity increased, but management believed that it had somewhat.
5. No one served as coordinator, and communications dropped substantially after the first few months, including feedback on suggestions.
6. No training programs existed for supervisors or committee reps. Some committees did not meet on a regular basis.
7. Supervisors were on the screening (plantwide) committee and dominated the discussions.
8. Indirect employees were not laid off anywhere near proportionally to direct labor employees.

9. Employees had much difficulty relating to the gainsharing with the fluctuations in volume and employment.
10. Because of volume fluctuations and pressures to improve performance, production control apparently deteriorated.
11. Because of erratic volume, trust in management had probably deteriorated.
12. Little emphasis was placed on communications, including calculation education, feedback of performance, follow-up of suggestions.
13. Inconsistent supervision was present throughout.
14. Misunderstandings occurred between the office and factory.
15. Bickering among management continued to expand.
16. Less than 50% of employees submitted suggestions, and follow-up procedures were frequently not completed.

Considering the above problems, there is little wonder why the employees voted the plan out in December, at the conclusion of the trial period. To compound the difficulties, raises were around 5% for the year and a new labor contract was to be negotiated early the following year. Management really made no attempt to salvage either their own or the employees' commitment to the system.

Obviously, this is a perfect example of where not to install a plan. Most of the variables in our model that we discussed above and were in the model presented in Chapter 1 were obviously violated. A perceived need to change does not make it occur, but things really do need to change in many areas. Management obviously missed the opportunity to make a major change.

A final note to this summary may be appropriate. In spite of the problems outlined above, operating profit for the first 11 months went from a negative $57,000 to a plus $114,000. Was the plan a total failure? Perhaps it did help to save the firm from extinction although no one would certainly consider it a success.

Contrasting Two Firms

The difficulty of measuring success or failure will now be considered by contrasting two firms, one a traditionally successful fairly high bonus-earning firm and the other in a poor market with a very competitive and low bonus-earning situation. The interesting conclusion, however, is that most unbiased observers would probably note the lower bonus gainsharing firm as having a much more successful plan when compared with the other. Firm A is the lower bonus-earning firm and Firm B is the higher one, as depicted in Table 9-2.

Financial and Bonus Performance.   To simplify the discussion, the presentation of these two cases is in summary form and limited to three

TABLE 9-2 Comparison of Firms A and B: Recent Three-Year Period

	FIRM A	FIRM B
Change in number of employees	(365) no change	(150) 5% increase
Man-hours per unit of output	24.2% increase	N/A
Scrap %	41.1% decrease	N/A
Sales change	51% increase	34% increase
Average bonus	6.1%	16.2%
Monthly average number of suggestions	29	N/A
Turnover	29.2% decrease	N/A
Wage increases (simple)	21.0%	27.3%
Profit changes (absolute)	471% (Beginning % on sales was 6%)	23.2%
Sales per employee	54% increase	34% increase
Financial productivity	not computed	13.8% increase (labor only)
Average assets	11.6% increase	28.6% increase

recent years where both behavioral and financial information is available. What follows is some financial and bonus-related information for the three-year period. Information not available is indicated by N/A.

When reviewing Table 9-2, one can see that Firm A is really doing much better in spite of the much lower bonus (6.1% vs. 16.2%). With the increase in information that is available, Firm A also places much more emphasis on measurement, goal setting, and accountability in general. Even though it is in a somewhat depressed industry compared with Firm B, its growth is obviously more impressive.

Behavioral Analysis. Since most contemporary gainsharing systems emphasize employee involvement and management commitment, we believe that it is important to evaluate this process through employee surveys. Table 9-3 summarizes some comparisons between Firms A and B on a few of the variables covered in a comprehensive survey.

In most areas, Firm A scores significantly higher on most questions than Firm B does—but not always, in spite of its significantly greater commitment to communications and involvement. Undoubtedly, the type of workforce has some impact on this effort as does the general wage level. Firm A does have a part-time coordinator while Firm B does not.

Since Firm A has had the plan in operation only about three years, it was decided to inquire into the operation of the plan in more depth. Considering the low level of wages the attitudes are quite good regarding the operation of the plan (see question 4, which was surprisingly high). Table 9-4 provides additional evidence supporting our model.

Unfortunately, quantitative surveys often do not "collect" as much of the general attitudes as one might like unless the number of questions is

151

TABLE 9-3 Two Gainsharing Firms—A Comparison of Attitudes

	PERCENT POSITIVE	
	Firm A: Successful	Firm B: Marginal
1. Is management willing to accept suggestions you make?	87%	86%
2. Does your supervisor ask your opinion when a problem comes up that involves your work?	75	66
3. How often do you offer suggestions about improving the operations of your job, work area, or department?	86	66
4. How important to you is the opportunity to participate in decisions concerning your job, work area, or department?	96	94
5. How well do you understand the Gainsharing Bonus calculation?	81	60
6. How well do you understand the Gainsharing Committee system?	80	65
7. How well do you understand the suggestion system?	86	78
8. Are suggestions processed quickly and efficiently?	40	47
9. Your committee representatives do everything they can to get suggestions from employees.	60	42
10. Your committee representatives put a lot of time and effort in their committee activities.	54	28
11. Committee representatives know what is expected of them.	78	54
12. Committee representatives keep us well-informed about the Plan (bonuses, problem areas, and so on).	63	59
13. Gainsharing encourages us to work as a team	87	79
14. Gainsharing encourages an individual to use his/her experience and knowledge on the job.	85	83
15. Most employees don't really care what the reports show, just if we have a bonus or not.	39	27
16. Many suggestions are put into effect immediately without being written upon a suggestion form.	46	56
17. The Gainsharing Plan helps improve communication and asking questions.	72	63
18. Cooperation between departments.	70	59
19. Communication between departments.	65	57
20. Trust and confidence in management is (mean).	3.3	2.4

expanded greatly. On both of the surveys, written comments were also requested regarding the general operation of the plan in general. Although the comments were obviously selected, they do reflect the general differences in attitudes that exist at the two firms. Firm A's employees are much more positive in spite of a poor market situation and low wages.

Firm A

1. It gives the men more incentive to work smarter. It gives you opportunity to use more of your imagination. Certainly the possibility of a little extra money each month is very nice. It brings management and bargaining employees closer together.

TABLE 9-4 Satisfaction, Supervision, and Scanlon Perceptions: Firm A

GENERAL SATISFACTION	PERCENT POSITIVE
1. All in all, how satisfied are you with your company?	87
2. All in all, how satisfied are you with your job?	88
3. All in all, how satisfied are you with your supervisor?	89
4. How satisfied would you say you are with your earnings?	46
5. How do outsiders feel about your company?	74

ABOUT YOUR SUPERVISOR	
6. To what extent do you have confidence and trust in your supervisor?	82
7. How well does your supervisor do planning and scheduling of your work?	78
8. How well does your supervisor handle the people side of his/her job (giving recognition, building teamwork, giving feedback, etc.)?	75

SCANLON OPERATION	
9. Participation has increased under the Gainsharing Plan.	83
10. The Gainsharing Plan helps improve cooperation.	80
11. The Gainsharing Plan helps improve communication.	72
12. The Gainsharing Plan helps increase quality	81
13. Management is committed to the plan.	81
14. Employees are committed to the plan.	77
15. The Gainsharing Plan is good for us here at _____.	88
16. The Gainsharing Plan has made this a more enjoyable place to work.	67
17. The calculation fairly reflects performance.	71

2. Gives you an extra paycheck. It rewards workers for their extra effort.

3. Creates cooperation between departments and individuals. Gives sense of contribution.

4. Helps to increase productivity. Decreases waste and increases quality. Encourages cooperation between employees. Monetary incentive for employees. Increases company profits.

5. Because the employees have begun to work together better and closer. The money every month.

6. Product quality, product quantity, efficiency of employees, and the bonus.

7. Because of the money, and sometimes people suggest things that really make your job easier.

8. Encourages high quality production with a monetary reward.

9. Makes everyone work together; makes the company more money and we produce better quality; helps the employee help himself; extra spending money.

10. Less waste, more involvement, more productivity, better communications and cooperation between departments, extra money if bonus is earned; company reputation is improving and climbing in ____ industry because of employee involvement.

153

Firm B

1. The gainsharing plan hasn't really been what I expected it to be. ____ management gives us the runaround when we have specific questions about the plan. Many times questions have been asked but never answered. It's times things change and bigger bonuses given.

2. I think that the people would be better informed about the plan so they can understand it and how the bonus works and what it actually is. I think there should be some concern about the high employee turnover.

3. One question I would like to know is this: Why is it that one month we put out an enormous amount of work and get very little bonus? Then the next month there is little work and a large bonus?

4. I do not believe ____ is paying us honestly and fairly what we deserve in the bonus; everything is taken out of the bonus if there is a loss, not taken out of the company profit.

5. I don't understand why the bonuses are down or up sometimes. My working harder than usual does not seem to affect the bonus one way or the other.

6. Management and employees must be more serious, with the company not just turning their heads on the employees' suggestions. ____ itself can be the best ____ manufacturers only if management would start using their heads and cooperate with the employees.

7. The bonus plan means that the management tells you what you get and that's it! You can't believe them.

8. It was never explained to the representatives why the bonuses suddenly dropped 1½ years ago from between 25% and 29% to between 0 and 9%.

9. Sometimes, if questions are asked at the meeting, there are never direct answers. They always are going to look into the matter. Later we still don't get answers.

10. The employees should be more informed about how the bonus plan works. It doesn't matter how hard you work, your bonus will never be as much as it should be at ____.

Knowledge of the Calculation. As part of the survey at both firms, an attempt was made to investigate how much each of the workforces understood about the calculation since some researchers have stated that understanding is important to building trust. Firm A had 14 true, false, don't-know questions on the calculation whereas Firm B had 11. The average respondent to Firm A marked 59% of the questions correctly whereas 49% of Firm B's were recorded correctly. This area is of importance to both firms but has received more attention in A.

Summary. This section evaluated and contrasted two firms. Firm A is much more committed to the gainsharing concept than is Firm B but the results do not always indicate the difference, perhaps because of conflicting variables such as pay, geographical area, and workforce characteristics. Employees of the firms obviously perceive many of the variables outlined in our model also to be important to gainsharing success.

NOTES

1. Robert A. Ruh, R.L. Wallace, and C.F. Frost, "Management Attitudes and the Scanlon Plan," *Industrial Relations*, 1973, pp. 282-288.

2. J.K. White, "The Scanlon Plan: Causes and Correlates of Success," *Academy of Management Journal* (June 1979): 292-312.

3. J.J. Jehring, "A Contrast Between Two Approaches to Total Systems Incentives," *California Management Review*, 1967, pp. 7-14.

4. Brian E. Moore, *A Plant-Wide Productivity Plan in Action: Three Years of Experience with the Scanlon Plan* (Washington, D.C.: National Commission on Productivity and Work Quality, May 1975).

5. Timothy L. Ross and G.M. Jones, "An Approach to Increased Productivity: The Scanlon Plan," *Financial Executives*, February 1972, pp. 23-29.

6. Anderson Ashburn, "Devising Real Incentives for Productivity," *American Machinist*, June 1978, pp. 115-30.

7. R. Helfgott, "Group Wage Incentives: Experience with the Scanlon Plan" (New York: Industrial Relations Counselors, Industrial Relations Memo, 1962).

8. Ashburn, "Devising Real Incentives."

9. Russell W. Davenport, "Enterprise for Everyman," *Fortune*, January 1950, pp. 50-58.

10. R.B. Gray, "The Scanlon Plan—A Case Study," *British Journal of Industrial Relations* 9: pp. 191-213.

11. Elbridge Puckett, "Productivity Achievements—A Measure of Success," in *The Scanlon Plan: A Frontier in Labor Management Cooperation*, ed. F.G. Lesieur (Cambridge, Mass.: Technology Press of M.I.T. and New York: Wiley, 1958).

12. Helfgott, "Group-Wage Incentives."

13. H. Thierry, "The Scanlon Plan: A Field Experimental Approach" (Symposium, 81st Annual Convention, American Psychological Association, 1973).

14. Moore, *A Plant-Wide Productivity Plan in Action: Three Years of Experience with the Scanlon Plan.*

15. Helfgott, "Group Wage Incentives."

16. Thierry, "The Scanlon Plan."

17. Ashburn, "Devising Real Incentives."

18. Herbert R. Northrup and H.A. Young, "The Causes of Industrial Peace Revisited," *Industrial and Labor Relations Review*, October 1968, pp. 31-47.

19. R.J. Doyle, "A New Look at the Scanlon Plan," *Management Accounting* p. 48 (September 1970).

20. William F. Whyte, *Money and Motivation* (New York: Harper and Brothers, 1955).

21. Moore, *A Plant-Wide Productivity Plan in Action: Three Years of Experience with the Scanlon Plan.*

22. Carl F. Frost, J.H. Wakely, and R.A. Ruh, The *Scanlon Plan for Organization Development: Identity, Participation, and Equity* (East Lansing: Michigan State University Press, 1974).

23. George Shultz, "Variations in Environment and the Scanlon Plan," in *The Scanlon Plan: A Frontier in Labor Management Cooperation*, ed. F.G. Lesieur (Cambridge, Mass.: Technology Press of M.I.T. and New York: Wiley, 1958).

24. A.J. Geare, "Productivity From Scanlon-Type Plans," *The Academy of Management Review*, July 1976, pp. 99-108.

25. Helfgott, "Group Wage Incentives."

26. Ibid.

27. Carl F. Frost, "The Scanlon Plan: Anyone for Free Enterprise?," *MSU Business Topics*, Winter 1978, pp. 25-33.

28. G.S. Burtnett, "A Study of Causal Relationships Between Organizational Variables and Personal Influence Variables During the Implementation of Scanlon Plans" (Ph.D. diss., Michigan State University, 1973).

29. Helfgott, "Group Wage Incentives."

30. Ashburn, "Devising Real Incentives."

31. George P. Shultz, "Worker Participation on Production Problems: A Discussion of Experience with the Scanlon Plan," *Personnel*, November 1951, pp. 209-11.

10

PG and the Future

by Timothy L. Ross and Brian E. Graham-Moore

Throughout this book, we have attempted to encourage the serious reader to critically evaluate the theory and evidence underlying productivity gainsharing. Its theoretical development is still extremely limited, but we are hopeful that this book will provide a significant major new contribution upon which to build. In the years to come, the country urgently needs considerably more work in both basic and applied theoretical gainsharing research.

Little doubt exists that most firms will never consider installation of productivity gainsharing. The extensive discussion of (1) organizational, (2) socio/cultural/institutional, (3) individual, and (4) financial variables, in Chapter 1, and discussion of why firms fail, in Chapter 9, should leave little room for doubt as to why many managements will not be directed toward a gainsharing plan. Most will never take the time and effort necessary to even consider such a system.

IMPEDIMENTS TO PG PROGRAMS

As part of a small study project, we asked top plant, group, and corporate managers in two firms knowledgeable about gainsharing why they did not believe more of their peers were actively studying gainsharing as a formalized strategy. Both had experienced strong encouragement and education attempts from corporate headquarters. Their response is condensed in the following 11 sections. We believe these opinions are indicative of true managerial concerns and probably illustrate why gainsharing will not be applied in all firms.

1. Why Pay For Something We Can Get From Good Management?   If everyone had this view, we wonder why the country's productivity growth has been so dismal the past few years.

2. Union Resistance.   Unions traditionally have not been strong advocates of gainsharing, probably because of feared loss of control or lack of knowledge or of fear it will be used in lieu of wage increments. This is slowly changing, although we are unaware of any national union advocating gainsharing at the plant level.

The United Auto Workers' union has long sought industrywide profit sharing as a wage supplement and has accepted productivity gainsharing in several locations.

Periodically, local union leaders still argue strongly against gainsharing. National, regional, or areawide labor contracts impede somewhat the application of gainsharing in the smaller unit basis, e.g., a plant. Obviously, where applicable, union leadership must be heavily involved in most situations for a plan to be successfully implemented.

3. Risk of Failure.   This is perceived as a particular problem for plants of a divisionalized firm. They often look upon gainsharing from a bonus standpoint and if conditions are not right, bonus earning opportunities may be limited or even nonexistent for some time. Unless there is a significant need to change because of poor performance or unless they are very successful and want to share the fruits of that success with employees, they are unlikely to be drawn toward gainsharing. Many managers do not realize that risk taking is one of the primary characteristics of a successful manager.

4. Lack of How-To Knowledge.   This will always be a problem in difficult measurement systems (e.g., pure service organizations). Until experiences are more widely known and research expands into new areas, we won't have any ready answers. Nevertheless, major improvements in accounting and information systems have been made in recent years, which should help in this area.

5. Management Style.   This could help installations of some systems and hurt others. For example, control-oriented firms might look upon Improshare very favorably but reject a scanlon orientation because of discomfort with employee involvement systems. Many other managers, although they do believe that employees at all levels contribute more to organizational success, do not believe that they do so unless forced into such a position. Supervisors often feel most threatened by gainsharing when involvement is required. This fear can be overcome through education and favorable experiences. Supervisory shifts are sometimes required. Many supervisors obviously will view gainsharing favorably by developing a better departmental team.

6. Lack of Divisional and Corporate Support. This is a major problem in some firms and nonexistent in others. Some firms do not want to establish a precedent for other units by allowing one to install gainsharing whereas others actively encourage with white papers, corporate task forces, staff support, seminars, references and so on. Very few have a corporate position paper on gainsharing, but more are developing such a document. Some firms have several layers of approval required, making it difficult for lower units to propose such plans. As with unions, however, the divisional and corporate resistance seems to be eroding nationally.

7. Costs Greater than Benefits. This is a problem, particularly in small organizations, since costs do not increase in proportion to size. For example, every organization must establish a calculation against which to measure performance. This frequently is more difficult in a small firm than a large one because small firms tend to have less sophisticated accounting systems. If an outside consultant is sought, these costs can be very significant in relation to net income for a small firm. Some corporate groups fund the earlier expenses but eventually the installing organization must pick up the charges. If small, they will not have sufficient personnel resources to complete much of the work and maintain the system.

8. What To Do With Existing Incentive Systems. These can range from individual, factory incentive systems to sales commissions to managerial bonus systems. Generally speaking, individual incentives are eliminated through some form of buyout. Sales commissions and managerial bonuses are continued although bonuses typically would not be paid on the incremental portion or a cap may be placed on sharing.

Individual incentives are thought to be somewhat inconsistent with group gainsharing because they emphasize what the individual can do for himself or herself whereas group gainsharing emphasizes what can be gained by working better together as a team. Rarely are individual incentives equitably maintained. If part of a union contract, obviously the union must be involved and committed to the elimination since it normally negotiates part or all of the incentive system. If existing at the time of installation, these systems can at times present thorny issues to resolve, but many firms do mesh the systems without major difficulty.

9. Inadequate Preparations. Still weak in our research methodology is how to establish whether a firm is a good candidate for installation and ultimate success. Our Chapter 1 should help significantly in this evaluation process. But what about the firm that is deemed inadequately prepared but still wants to proceed? How does it prepare itself? Each of the major problem areas addressed in Chapter 1 must be carefully reviewed and upgraded, whether it be in the broad areas of management commitment, employee identification with problems, financial system sophistication, or any others. Each may take considerable time and resources.

Frankly, many managers are unwilling to make such an investment and will drop gainsharing. The normal implementation time is probably around one to two years, with impatient managements losing interest before the preparatory work is completed if the plan is to be oriented toward employee involvement. Such time lags are not required, but normally occur; if much shorter time periods are necessary, Improshare should be seriously considered without the involvement aspects.

10. Difficulty with Devising Calculations. Obviously some situations will result in limitations in calculation alternatives. For example, a pure service firm could probably not use Improshare but could use budgets or multicost. Multicost or value-added formulas resolve most of the problems in job order shops. Rarely is a calculation impossible to develop if management is determined.

11. Ineffective Situations. If a participative management approach is oriented toward employer involvement, some observers believe that it has difficulty being effective in crisis situations, with incompetent employees, and when employees value strong direction. These opinions have not been validated, but they should be considered as topics of further research.

These and still others are strong arguments frequently cited by some managers against productivity gainsharing. They obviously can be overcome as many sucesssful managers have found and could be used to argue in favor of PG. We believe that the arguments in favor of PG far outweigh those against if the firm has the appropriate profile (see Chapter 1).

THE FUTURE AND PG

Even given the present level of theory development, we believe that the current growth trends in productivity gainsharing will continue and perhaps accelerate in the near future. We note several reasons for this.

Many business and government leaders publicly proclaim the great importance of productivity growth in maintaining a satisfactory standard of living without major inflation. In 1982, President Reagan formed a blue-ribbon National Productivity Council to address the declining productivity growth rate. Gainsharing surely will become part of the Council's long-term matrix of endorsed systems. No other system incorporates the behaviorally intrinsic variables of employee involvement, recognition, problem identification, and accountability with the extrinsic rewards of gainsharing. Although we have provided some of the limited statistics on declining national productivity growth in this book, the literature is saturated with causal analyses and prognoses of gloom and doom. Gainsharing will undoubtedly play an increasing role in helping to reverse these trends if for no other reasons that more managers are behaviorally attuned to employee involvement and are motivated toward sharing the financial benefits of any productivity increase.

Better references are available today. In the past, few publishers of books or editors of journals were willing to accept articles on gainsharing. This is no longer true. Greater national need is one reason, coupled with the expansion of principles that underlie most long-term successful applications of the various systems. Many more researchers are starting to become involved in gainsharing. International exposure and application are bound to grow as other industrialized countries realize that the Japanese have a fairly elaborate system for sharing the productivity improvements with employees. Even considering the references available, we are perplexed by the large numbers of managers who have not heard of gainsharing. Many of the remainder perceive all of the plans as emphasizing the group incentive aspect much greater than the quality of work life variables.

More flexible formulas are now available. In earlier years, many managers perceived the need to establish fairly common productivity-sharing calculations. Today, calculations are extremely flexible to varying conditions with most organizations customizing each one to fit their own needs at a particular time. Calculations have been designed or are being developed for processing and job order manufacturing concerns, engineering firms, banks, hospitals, insurance companies, state and city organizations, to name a few. They may be based on performance productivity measures such as physical measures of output and input or on financial productivity measures close to and including profit and return on investment. Some approach the problem from a prospective or targeted productivity performance. We believe that this expansion of calculations will keep PG applications spread to many more different types of organizations.

Our PG knowledge and experience are much greater today. Perhaps more gainsharing systems have been installed during the past three years than in the entire history of the three commonly cited systems (scanlon, Rucker, and Improshare). The expansion that Joe Scanlon thought would develop in the 1950s is now starting.

Emphasis is switching fairly rapidly away from confrontation within organizations to a more cooperative environment. Because of the need to change, both unions and managements—of unionized and nonunionized firms—perceive much to be gained from developing a more cooperative climate. This is the result of numerous changes including the realization that the least costly capacity is that which is currently available. Competitors, both domestic and foreign, are being identified as the enemy rather than the forces within the organization. Management is now starting to indicate a willingness to spend the time and money to develop that identity. The current emphasis on Quality Control Circles and other employee-oriented systems are also indicative of that increased emphasis on cooperation and employee involvement with gainsharing being just one step beyond.

Total organizational approaches to organizational development make more sense today as we become more interdependent, automated, and constantly changing. The old inertia against change will leave the slow-moving organizations by the wayside in the 1980s, and increasing numbers of managers will likely perceive the goal-oriented, employee-involvement gainsharing plans to be desirable systems toward which to move. Many

Quality Control Circle firms will probably evolve toward gainsharing because of pressures to share the financial benefits of improvements without considering the intra-organizational committee linking systems that underlie many gainsharing firms.

We have more successes today. Plans seem to be better installed, monitored, and evaluated. Although conjecture is obviously admitted, the long-term success rate is probably approaching the 65% to 70% range. Some of the firms that drop their systems because of economic conditions would prefer to manage in a participative style and eventually reconsider their systems. Obviously, firms lose their plans for a variety of reasons, including those outlined in the model discussed in Chapter 9. Most observers believe that a long-term success rate of, say, 65% is outstanding considering some installation situations and monitoring techniques utilized.

We note with some pride that popular books such as William Ouchi's *Theory Z* espouse decision making based on the cooperation and participation of the Japanese experience.[1] Without question, making explicit a philosophy that includes the objectives of an organization as well as the constraints placed on the organization by social and economic forces is a step toward a new form of management. While it may be called Theory Z, Joe Scanlon might smile quietly if he were still with us.

Apparently, some American managers predate the Japanese if we look to the past 30 years. For example, Richard Pascale and William Athos, in *The Art of Japanese Management,* express the belief that the superiority of Japanese management is explained by its managerial beliefs, assumptions, perceptions, style, and skill.[2] Ouchi, who mentions scanlon plans as compatible with Z philosophy, maintains that involved workers are the key to productivity. Well, if Japanese managers are ahead of American ones, then scanlon managers have been ahead of both the Japanese and their fellow Americans. It is held by new scholars that Japanese managers practice interdependence. That is, the human resource of a corporation is regarded as a collaborator—not as an extension of a machine. If managerial style is a functional factor in Japanese firms, then PG firms with high involvement reflect a kind of style that is open, problem-oriented, yet conducive to future relationships (no win/lose or face saving).

Where does this leave us? In Figure 1–2, we indicated that some newer forms of PG are evolving and being designed. They are a logical extension of the development of PG since the 1930s. It is very likely that we will see examples of these new forms in the 1980s. The American workforce has continually upgraded itself. The forces that produce high-quality workers and managers will inevitably produce newer and better forms of PG.

In fact, while some gainsharing firms may practice more pseudo-participation than truly believing in it as a way of worklife, a few firms are starting to adopt what might be considered new and different forms of PG.

Two commonly cited examples are Donnelley Mirrors and Herman Miller. Both have innovative and advanced calculations. They also have developed involvement systems and management commitment that are likely to set the standard in the future for newer forms of PG.

Figure 10-1 illustrates results collected by the U.S. General Accounting Office in a survey of gainsharing firms.[3] Of note is the fact that many PG firms recognize that nonmonetary benefits are clearly associated with successful experiences. Better teamwork, increased job satisfaction, less resistance to change, and closer identification with the firm go hand in hand with the findings of this GAO survey. It is not surprising that improved labor-management relations, fewer grievances, less absenteeism, and reduced turnover are associated with gainsharing firms.

We are enthusiastic over and encouraged by recent growth in productivity gainsharing interest and application. The General Accounting office study concluded by saying, ". . . [w]e have found that when properly

FIGURE 10-1 Nonmonetary Benefits of Productivity Sharing Programs. [Source: U.S. General Accounting Office, *Productivity Sharing Programs: Can They Contribute to Productivity Improvements?* AFMD-81-22, (Gaithersburg, Md.: U.S. General Accounting Office, 1981) p. 17.]

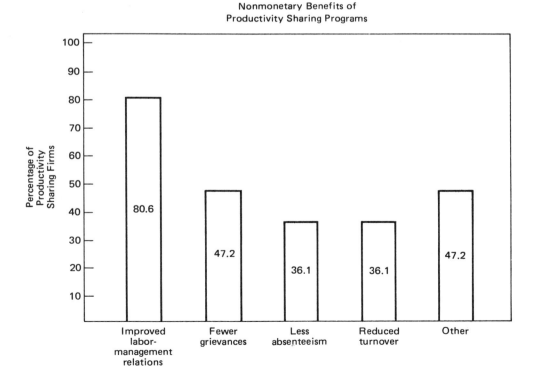

Nonmonetary Benefits of
Productivity Sharing Programs

implemented and administered, productivity sharing plans can effectively contribute to improved productivity." We agree with this statement and believe that its future is bright. We hope this book will help those who are interested in both conducting research in and implementing productivity gainsharing.

NOTES

1. W. G. Ouchi, *Theory Z: How American Business Can Meet the Japanese Challenge* (Reading, Mass.: Addison-Wesley, 1981).

2. Richard T. Pascale and Anthony G. Athos, *The Art of Japanese Management* (New York: Simon and Schuster, 1981).

3. U.S. General Accounting Office, *Productivity Sharing Programs: Can They Contribute to Productivity Improvements?* AFMD–81–22 (Gaithersburg, Md.: U.S. General Accounting Office, March 3, 1981).

Glossary of PG Terms

Allowed Labor Formula: A calculation similar to the Improshare formula. The base ratio equals the allowed labor activity multiplied by the allowed wage with a provision for all indirect labor costs. (Scanlon)

Base Productivity Factor: The relationship in the base period between the actual hours worked by all employees and the value of the work in man-hours produced by these employees. This value is determined by the measurement standards used in the base period, or;

$$BPF = \frac{\text{Direct labor hours} + \text{indirect labor hours}}{\text{Total standard value hours (Improshare)}}.$$

Base Ratio: The total personnel costs divided by the sales value of production (sales +/- change inventory valued at cost or sales price). The original single ratio of Joseph Scanlon, often referred to as the single ratio of labor. (Scanlon)

Bonus Reserve: A portion of the gross bonus set aside to compensate for deficit months. At the end of each scanlon year, any reserve is distributed. Any year-end deficit is absorbed by the firm. (Scanlon, Rucker)

Source: Adapted from Brian E. Moore, *Sharing the Gains of Productivity* (Scarsdale, New York: Work in America Institute with Pergamon Press, 1982). The authors have inserted the type of PG plan with which these terms are usually associated. Where there is no PG plan mentioned, the terms are general to all applications.

Buy-Back Principle: Workers receive a cash payment for productivity gains they achieve over established ceilings. For this bonus, management has the right to change the product standard. (Improshare)

Ceiling: A productivity limit. Productivity exceeding the ceiling can be banked and eventually brought back to the employees in the form of a cash payment—the buy-back. (Improshare)

Fixed Payroll: On a current basis, the total employment costs for the human resources whose time does not vary directly with annual production volume.

Improshare: Invented by Mitchell Fein, the name is an acronym for Improved Productivity Through Sharing. Past average productivity determines the Base Productivity Factor (BPF). The BPF is multiplied by standard hours to produce Improshare hours. The actual hours required to produce acceptable results less the Improshare hours can create a bonus that is split 50–50 by management and workers. (Improshare)

Memo of Understanding: A document that defines the PG plan—especially in regard to defining the bonus calculation and any involvement system responsibilities. (Scanlon)

Multi-Cost Formula: A calculation that includes materials and other costs with the labor cost, which is then divided by the sales value of production. While based, like profit sharing on success of the firm, it has many advantages over profit sharing since it is productivity (or output/input) related. (Scanlon)

Participating Payroll: Those employees sharing in the bonus pay-out—typically all employees (managers and workers) less the sales force and probationary employees. (Scanlon, Rucker)

Production (or Departmental) Committee: A committee composed of employee and management representatives that considers productivity-improving suggestions from its area. It refers all suggestions not within its realm of responsibility to the screening committee for review and, perhaps, broader implementation. (Scanlon)

Production Value: The difference between the market value of goods and the material cost and services used in producing these goods equal to the value added by the firm. (Rucker)

Productivity Gainsharing: Usually, the measurement of labor productivity divided by some measure of the results of that labor such as sales value of production, units produced, or the production value. A difference in the ratio between past expected productivity and actual productivity that indicates more of the denominator for less numerator and thus creates a bonus.

$$\text{Expected: } \frac{\text{Labor cost}}{\begin{array}{c}\text{Sales Value of Production}\\ \text{Units produced, or}\\ \text{Production Value}\end{array}} = .30$$

$$\text{Actual: } \frac{\text{Labor cost}}{\begin{array}{c}\text{Sales Value of Production}\\ \text{Units produced, or}\\ \text{Production Value}\end{array}} = .28$$

Therefore: E – A or 30 – 28 = 2 or Bonus

Profit Sharing: A system under which the firm pays compensation to employees in addition to their regular wages, based upon the profits of the company. While not output/input related, it is usually based on a definite formula specifying how much of the profit is to be distributed and how it is to be computed, usually at the end of the fiscal year.

Quality Circles: This team-building concept involves small groups of departmental work leaders and line operators who have volunteered to spend time helping solve various departmental problems. The groups are taught problem-solving techniques and how to present their solutions to management. These circles are similar to scanlon production committees.

Rucker Committee: These committees are composed of employee and management representatives whose purpose is to improve communication between workers and management about suggestions, problems, and solutions. (Rucker)

Rucker Plan: A productivity gainsharing program that measures economic productivity as the index of the overall effectiveness of a work group. Its goal is to maximize the output value of production (value added) for a given input value of payroll. (Rucker)

Rucker Standard: The percentage of the production value paid out in wages and benefits to nonexempt employees. It is calculated by dividing variable payroll costs by the production value.

$$\text{Rucker Standard} = \frac{\text{Variable Payroll Costs}}{\text{Production Value}}$$

If costs are less than this standard, a bonus is earned.

Sales Value of Production: The actual month's sales, plus or minus the inventory. (Scanlon or Rucker)

Scanlon Single Ratio Formula: One of the original productivity gainsharing formulas, the base ratio

$$\frac{\text{Costs}}{\text{Sales value of inventory}} = \text{the norm}$$

The norm is the expected relationship between costs and sales value of inventory. Actual personnel costs are subtracted from expected to create a bonus or deficit. (Scanlon)

Scanlon Plan: An organizationwide productivity improvement plan designed to increase productivity through greater efficiency and reduced costs. The basic elements of the plan are the philosophy and practice of cooperation, the involvement system, and formulas to measure increased productivity and distribute bonuses. (Scanlon)

Screening Committee: Composed of representatives from employees and management, it reviews and disposes of suggestions from the production committees, reviews bonus results, and discusses the economics of the firm.

Split Ratio Formula: A calculation composed of two or more base ratios of payroll costs divided by value of production, with each calculated for a product line or buy-outs. (Scanlon)

Standard Time: The time, usually established by a time and motion study, required for a worker to perform a specific operation without undue fatigue. Incentive earnings are gained when the worker produces in less than the standard time. (Improshare)

Standard Value Hours: The amount of time needed to produce the finished goods. It is calculated by multiplying the number of finished goods by the time needed to produce each of the goods. (Improshare)

Suggestion Systems: Employee involvement programs that provide employees the opportunity to give ideas to management that can increase the effectiveness and efficiency of the firm.

Value-Added Formula: A formula that is similar to the Rucker formula. The value of production (adjustments) less outside purchases (materials, etc.) multiplied by the historically determined base ratio to equal the allowed labor cost. Then, the allowed cost minus actual cost equals the increase or decrease to productivity. (Scanlon)

Variable Payroll: Total employment costs on current basis, for people whose time input varies directly with annual production. Also, these are costs that one may want to control on a directly variable basis with current volume.

Variable Purchases: Costs to procure goods and services that are consumed during production. These vary with the level of production. Management wants employees to try to conserve them by seeing their impact on the bonus; especially applicable to the Rucker Plan.

Work-Hour Standard: The average number of man-hours required to produce a finished product as calculated by dividing the total man-hours by units produced. May also be based on engineered time standards.

Index

NOW ... *Announcing these other fine books from Prentice-Hall—*

To order these books, just complete the convenient order form below and mail to **Prentice-Hall, Inc., General Publishing Division, Attn. Addison Tredd, Englewood Cliffs, N.J. 07632**

ORGANIZATION DEVELOPMENT: A Total Systems Approach to Positive Change in Any Business, by Karl Albrecht. Presents a simple systems model to, among other things, create a climate for candid problem solving, develop task forces, interject the strategic planning process, and more.

$18.95 hardcover

THE ART OF LEADERSHIP: Skill-Building Techniques That Produce Results, by Lin Bothwell. An award-winning creative writer who has trained more than 8,000 executives shows how to improve leadership skills in such areas as communications, time management, career planning, problem solving, and decision making.

$9.95 paperback, $18.95 hardcover

Title	Author	Price*

Subtotal _____

Sales Tax (where applicable) _____

Postage & Handling (75¢/book) _____

Total $ _____

Please send me the books listed above. Enclosed is my check ☐ Money order ☐ or, charge my VISA ☐ MasterCard ☐ Account # _____

Credit card expiration date _____

Name _____

Address _____

City _____ State _____ Zip _____

Prices subject to change without notice. Please allow 4 weeks for delivery.